SCIENCE ACTIVITIES

EVERYDAY CHEMISTRY

VOLUME 2

Lisa Magloff

GROLIER
EDUCATIONAL

Published 2002 by Grolier Educational
Sherman Turnpike,
Danbury, Connecticut 06816

FOR BROWN PARTWORKS

Project editor:	Lisa Magloff
Deputy editor:	Jane Scarsbrook
Text editors:	Caroline Beattie, Mukul Patel
Designers:	Joan Curtis, Alison Gardener
Picture researcher:	Liz Clachan
Illustrations:	Darren Awuah, Mark Walker
Index:	Kay Ollerenshaw
Design manager:	Lynne Ross
Production manager:	Matt Weyland
Managing editor:	Bridget Giles
Editorial director:	Anne O'Daly
Consultant:	Donald R. Franceschetti, PhD University of Memphis

Printed and bound in Hong Kong

Set ISBN 0-7172-5608-1
Volume ISBN 0-7172-5610-3

Library of Congress Cataloging-in-Publication Data
Science Activities / Grolier Educational
        p. cm.
    Includes index.
    Contents: v.1. Electricity and magnetism—v.2. Everyday Chemistry—v.3. Force and motion—v.4. Heat and energy—v.5. Inside matter—v.6. Light and color—v.7. Our Environment—v.8. Sound and hearing—v.9. Using materials—v.10. Weather and climate.
ISBN 0-7172-5608-1 (set : alk.paper)—ISBN 0-7172-5609-X (v.1 : alk. paper)—
ISBN 0-7172-5610-3 (v.2 : alk. paper)—ISBN 0-7172-5611-1 (v.3 : alk. paper)—ISBN
0-7172-5612-X (v.4 : alk. paper)—ISBN 0-7172-5613-8 (v.5 : alk. paper)—ISBN
0-7172-5614- 6 (v.6 : alk. paper)—ISBN 0-7172-5615-4 (v.7 : alk. paper)—ISBN
0-7172-5616-2 (v.8 : alk. paper)—ISBN 0-7172-5617-0 (v.9 : alk. paper)—ISBN
0-7172-5618-9 (v.10 : alk. paper)
    1. Science—Study and teaching—Activity programs—Juvenile literature. [1. Science—Experiments. 2. Experiments] I. Grolier Educational (Firm)

LB1585.S335 2002
507.1'2—dc21

2001040519

ABOUT THIS SET

Science Activities gives children a chance to explore fascinating topics from the world of science using the same methods that professional scientists use to solve problems. This set introduces young scientists to the scientific method by focusing on the importance of planning experiments, conducting them in a rigorous fashion so that a fair test can be carried out, recording all the stages, and organizing and analyzing the data to draw conclusions. Readers will have the chance to conduct exciting and innovative hands-on activities and to learn how to record and analyze their experiments and results in a variety of ways.

Every volume of *Science Activities* contains 10 step-by-step experiments, along with follow-up activities that encourage readers to find out more about the subject. The activities are explained and enhanced with detailed introductory and analysis sections. Colorful photos illustrate each activity, and every book is packed full of pictures and illustrations explaining the details of each topic.

By working fun and educational experiments into the context of the scientific method, anyone using this set can get a feel for how professional scientists go about their work. Most importantly, just have fun!

PICTURE CREDITS
(t=top; b=bottom; l=left; r=right)

Corbis: 49 (b), Betteman 57, Owen Franken 33, Michelle Garrett 6, Richard Hamilton Smith 50, Jacqui Hurst 39 (l), Michael Neveux 12, Liba Taylor 17, Nick Wheeler 38; **Ecoscene:** Cooper 19, PT 39 (r); **Image Bank:** Alan Becker 37, Elyse Lewin Studio Inc. 28, Jeff Hunter front cover, 18, Pertrified Collection 44, Harald Sund 55, JH Pete Carmichael 51(b), Peter Cade 51 (t); **NASA:** Kennedy Space Center 45; **Science Photo Library:** 61 (t), Moredun Animal Health 49 (t), Sinclair Stammers 61 (b), Andrew Syred 13, 23, 56; **Sylvia Cordaiy:** John Farmer 10; **Travel Ink:** Colin Marshall.

CONTENTS

VOLUME 2
EVERYDAY CHEMISTRY

INTRODUCTION

Chemical reactions occur all the time, all around you, and inside you. Plants growing, iron rusting, gas burning in car engines, your saliva and stomach juices digesting your food—all these processes involve chemical changes.

All matter in the universe is made up of basic building blocks called atoms. Matter that contains only one kind of atom is called an element. Gold, iron, and carbon are all elements. There are 92 elements that occur naturally. Other substances, called compounds, contain atoms of more than one element bonded (joined) together. Water, salt, sugar, the polyethylene in plastic bags, and the DNA in your cells are all compounds.

Most matter consists of atoms bonded together to form molecules or crystals.

■ *Sulfur is sometimes called the yellow element. It is widely distributed naturally and was once known as brimstone.*

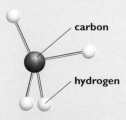

carbon

hydrogen

■ *Hydrogen and carbon atoms form this molecule of methane.*

A molecule is the smallest unit of a substance that can exist on its own. For example, each molecule of oxygen gas contains two oxygen atoms. Water molecules contain one oxygen and two hydrogen atoms. Many solid substances such as metals, diamond, and salt (sodium chloride) are crystals—regular arrangements of atoms with distinct shapes and sharp edges. Chemists study the properties of elements and compounds and the changes (called chemical reactions) that they undergo.

There are three major branches of chemistry. Organic chemistry deals with carbon and its compounds. Carbon is unique because it forms vast numbers of compounds, including ones that make up living things. Inorganic chemistry looks at all the other elements. Physical chemistry studies the changes that occur during chemical reactions.

The chemist's most important tool is the periodic table, which contains the elements arranged in order of the number of protons (or electrons) in their atoms. Elements that have similar properties are found close together on the table. Chemists can use the periodic table to predict the properties of an element before confirming them by experiment.

The experiments in this book will introduce important chemical reactions that take place all around you or inside you and other living things.

INSIDE THE ATOM

Atoms are made up of extremely small particles called protons, neutrons, and electrons. Protons have a positive electric charge. Electrons have a negative electric charge. Neutrons have no charge. The protons and neutrons are bound tightly together to form the nucleus of the atom, which is about one hundred thousandth as wide as the whole atom. The electrons move around outside this nucleus. Atoms have the same number of electrons as protons, so the charges balance. Atoms gain, lose, or share electrons in chemical reactions, but the nucleus does not change. Nuclear changes can only be produced with a much greater supply of energy than that involved in chemical reactions.

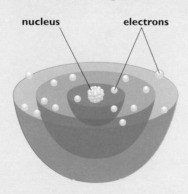
nucleus   electrons

Structure of an atom.

When atoms combine to make compounds, they arrange themselves in particular patterns, upsetting the balance between positive and negative charges. To form a compound, an atom may lose one or more electrons. If an electron is lost, the protons and electrons no longer balance. The positive charge is greater than the negative. An atom may also gain electrons. In either case the atom becomes electrically charged and is known as an ion. There are two types of ion. When electrons are lost, the atom becomes a positively charged particle called a cation. If electrons are gained, the atom becomes a negatively charged anion.

The attractive forces between the electrons and protons hold the atoms together in "bonds." Atoms share electrons in a "covalent" bond and transfer electrons in an "ionic" bond.

The good science guide

Science is not only a collection of facts—it is the process that scientists use to gather information. Follow this good science guide to get the most out of each experiment.

• Carry out each experiment more than once. This prevents accidental mistakes skewing the results. The more times you carry out an experiment, the easier it will be to see if your results are accurate.
• Decide how you will write down your results. You can use a variety of different methods, such as descriptions, diagrams, tables, charts, and graphs. Choose the methods that will make your results easy to read and understand.
• Be sure to write your results down as you are doing the experiment. If one of the results seems very different from the others, it could be because of a problem with the experiment that you should fix immediately.
• Drawing a graph of your results can be very useful because it helps fill in the gaps in your experiment. Imagine, for example, that you plot time along the bottom of the graph and temperature up the side. If you measure the temperature ten times, you can put the results on the graph as dots. Draw a straight line or a smooth curved line through all the dots. You can now estimate what happened in between each dot, or measurement, by picking any point along the line and reading the time and temperature for that point from the sides of the graph.
• Learn from your mistakes. Some of the most exciting findings in science came from an unexpected result. If your results do not tally with your predictions, try to find out why.
• You should always be careful when carrying out or preparing any experiment, whether it is dangerous or not. Make sure you know the safety rules before you start working.
• Never begin an experiment until you have talked to an adult about what you are going to do.

ACTIVITY 1
ACIDS AND BASES

Acids and bases are "opposite" types of compounds that react together to form water and a salt. Acids, bases, and salts are all around us—vinegar is an acid, baking soda is a base, and table salt is an example of a salt.

The word "acid" comes from the Latin *acidus*, which means sharp. Those acids that are safe to consume are sharp or sour in taste. Grapes contain tartaric acid, and carbonated drinks contain carbonic acid, which is produced when carbon dioxide gas dissolves in water. Car batteries contain a strong acid called sulfuric acid, which burns skin, and our stomachs contain a strong acid called hydrochloric acid, which helps the process of digestion so our bodies can absorb nutrients in food.

Acids contain hydrogen; when they dissolve in water, these hydrogen atoms form hydrogen ions (symbol H^+). A hydrogen ion is a hydrogen atom that has lost an electron and is left with a positive

■ *Citrus fruits like lemons, limes, and oranges contain citric acid, which gives them their sour taste. Citric acid is also added to many different foods during processing.*

charge. When a weak acid, like citric acid, is dissolved in water, only a small number of hydrogen atoms dissolve to form ions. In a strong acid most of the hydrogen atoms dissolve to form ions. Strong acids are used in industry to "etch" (eat away) metals, for example, in computer chip manufacture.

A base is a substance that dissolves in water to form negatively charged hydroxide ions (symbol OH^-). Strong bases dissolve to form many ions, while weak bases form fewer ions. Like strong acids,

Acid and base molecules

Molecules of acidic compounds contain hydrogen, which they release in the form of ions (hydrogen atoms that have lost an electron) when they dissolve in water. Hydrogen ions give acids their corrosive properties, but the ions only exist in solution, so only dissolved acids are corrosive.

Basic compounds dissolve in water to form negative hydroxide ions. The other part of the base is often a metal such as sodium or magnesium. A base that can dissolve in water is called an alkali. Strong bases are dangerous since they react with fats such as those in human tissue.

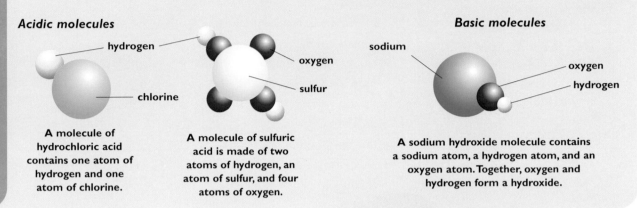

Acidic molecules

hydrogen

oxygen

sulfur

chlorine

A molecule of hydrochloric acid contains one atom of hydrogen and one atom of chlorine.

A molecule of sulfuric acid is made of two atoms of hydrogen, an atom of sulfur, and four atoms of oxygen.

Basic molecules

sodium

oxygen

hydrogen

A sodium hydroxide molecule contains a sodium atom, a hydrogen atom, and an oxygen atom. Together, oxygen and hydrogen form a hydroxide.

strong bases are dangerous in concentrated solutions. Weak bases are safe to touch and often feel slippery. Baking soda is a weak base. Sodium hydroxide, an industrial chemical, is a strong base.

Acids and bases react together to form new substances. Hydrogen hydroxide ions combine to form water (H_2O). Water is neither an acid nor a base—chemists say that it is "neutral." When acids and bases dissolve, other ions are formed too, and these can combine with each other to make a substance called a salt. Generally, salts are neutral. When hydrochloric acid and sodium hydroxide react, they form sodium chloride (common salt) and water.

The strength of acids and bases is measured on the pH scale. The scale runs from 1 to 14 and is a measure of the number of dissolved hydrogen ions. A solution with pH 1 contains a high proportion of hydrogen atoms and is a strong acid. A pH of 14 means the solution has few hydrogen ions and many hydroxide ions, and so is a strong base. A pH of 7 means equal numbers of hydrogen and hydroxide ions—a neutral solution. Water has a pH of 7.

Acids and bases occur in a delicate balance in nature—if the pH of a pond changes too much, plants and animals in it will die. There is a delicate balance inside our bodies, too—most of the reactions for life can only take place within a narrow pH range.

Indicators

There are various ways to measure the pH of substances, and one of the most common is to use an indicator. An indicator is a substance that changes color depending on the strength of the acid or base. You might have already used one type of indicator called litmus paper—acids turn blue litmus red, and bases turn red litmus blue. You can also use an indicator called pH paper, which turns different colors (see below) depending on the strength of the acid or base it is dipped into.

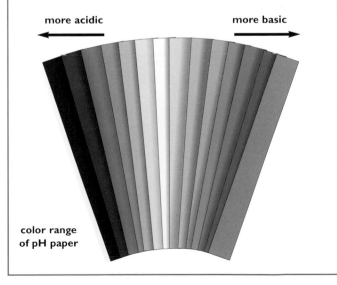

more acidic

more basic

color range of pH paper

Making an Indicator

Goals

1. **Make your own indicator solution.**
2. **Use the indicator to test liquids to see if they are acidic, neutral, or basic.**

What you will need:

- red cabbage
- stainless steel or enamel pan or microwave casserole dish
- 1 quart (0.9l) water
- stove, microwave, or hot plate
- knife and cutting board
- measuring cup
- strainer
- vinegar and baking soda
- teaspoon
- 2 jars

1 Chop up the cabbage. Put the chopped cabbage in a covered pot with the water, and boil it for 30 minutes.

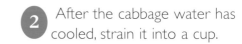

2 After the cabbage water has cooled, strain it into a cup.

Safety tip

Be careful when using hot water and knives. Always have an adult present to supervise and to help you.

Acid rain

All rainwater is slightly acidic because carbon dioxide in the air dissolves in rain to form carbonic acid. Too much acid in rain damages plants, animals, and buildings. When fossil fuels like coal and oil are burned, they release acidic gases into the air that dissolve in water in the clouds to make strong acids. They then fall to the ground as acid rain.

3 Pour ¼ cup of cabbage juice into a jar. Add ½ teaspoon baking soda to the jar and stir. Note what color the water turns.

Troubleshooting

What if the indicator does not change color?

If you are testing a liquid that is a dark color, such as grape juice, it will be difficult to see the color change. This type of indicator only works well with clear or light-colored liquids and dissolved powders.

4 Pour ¼ cup of cabbage juice into a jar, then add ½ teaspoon vinegar. Now what color does the water turn?

5 Now pour the contents of the vinegar jar into the baking soda jar, and observe what happens.

FOLLOW-UP Making an indicator

You can also collect rainwater if you place a jar out in the open on a rainy day, and measure its pH. If you measure the pH of different drinks, you should notice that many of the liquids we commonly drink, like soda, coffee, tea, and juice, are acidic.

You can also test the acidity of rainwater. Place a jar out in the open on a rainy day, and collect rainwater. Test it with the indicator. Is it acidic? If it is, you may have acid rain where you live. You may also learn a lot by testing the water in various places, like your home, your school, and in public buildings. What about swimming pool water? Is some drinking water more acidic or more basic than others? Water should ideally be close to neutral. If it is not, it may not be good to drink.

▶ *You can use your homemade indicators to test the acidity of a variety of liquids.*

ANALYSIS
Acids and bases

Red cabbage contains pigments called anthocyanins, which change color depending on the concentration of hydrogen ions in solution. The cabbage indicator will generally turn red in the presence of an acid, and purple or dark blue in the presence of a base.

Try testing the indicator on a common antacid medicine. There is normally some acid in our stomachs that helps us digest food. But sometimes, especially if we are upset or under stress, our stomach makes too much acid, which starts to digest the stomach lining. This produces indigestion and can cause a sore called an ulcer. Antacid medicines help neutralize excess stomach acid. The main ingredient in milk of magnesia is magnesium hydroxide. What color would you expect it to turn the indicator? Now test your prediction.

■ *A moor covered in heathers. The color of flowers like heathers depends partly on the acidity of the soil.*

One laboratory technique that uses indicators is titration. During a titration one reactant is added drop by drop to the other until the indicator changes color, marking the end of the reaction. You can perform a titration using your indicator to find when an acid and base completely neutralize each other. To start, observe the color change when cabbage juice is added to a small amount of acid, like vinegar. Then, using a dropper, add a small amount of base, such as window cleaner (which contains ammonia), to the cabbage juice and acid mixture. When the solution turns purple again, you have added just enough base to neutralize the acid. The more drops of base it takes to turn the solution purple, the stronger the acid.

Dissolving ions

An acidic solution is one in which an acid has dissolved to form lots of hydrogen ions (H^+), while a basic solution is one in which a base has dissolved to form lots of hydroxide (OH^-) ions.

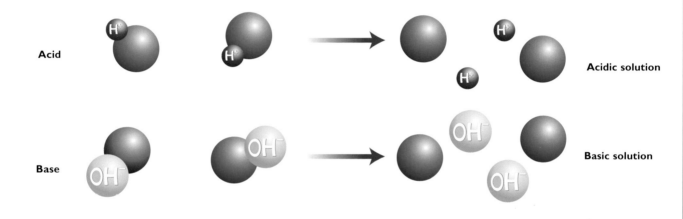

A solution with a low pH is one that has a large number of hydrogen ions (H^+), while a solution with a high pH has a large number of hydroxide (OH^-) ions.

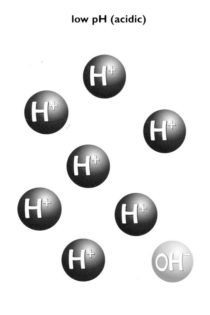

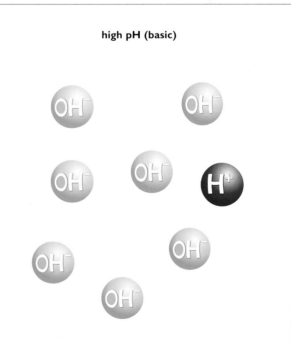

low pH (acidic)

high pH (basic)

ACTIVITY 2
SALTY SOAP

Table salt, plaster of Paris, bath salts, and soap are all examples of types of compounds called salts. Some salts dissolve in water, while others do not.

Have you ever wondered why using soap and water gets you cleaner than washing with just water, or why soap never gets dirty? Water can dissolve many substances, but it cannot dissolve grease. To dissolve grease so that it can be washed away, the grease has to be broken down. Soap breaks up the grease and allows it to dissolve in water. It is able to do this because it is a salt.

You are already familiar with one salt— sodium chloride (NaCl). That is the chemical formula for the salt that you sprinkle on your food. Sodium chloride dissolves easily in water. It occurs in seawater,

Soap is used with more enthusiasm now than in any other period of its 3,000-year history.

from which it is extracted by evaporation. It also occurs in solid form as rock salt or as a crystal called halite. Salt is necessary to all animal life, and people use it to flavor food and preserve food.

When scientists talk about salts, they are not just talking about the common salt on your dinner table. Chemically speaking, salts are compounds made of a metal and a nonmetal. Salts are made when an acid and a base react together. For example, when hydrochloric acid (HCl, a strong acid) and sodium hydroxide (NaOH, a strong base) are mixed together, ions of sodium metal combine with chloride ions to make sodium chloride (NaCl). The reaction also produces water (H_2O).

Soap is made from animal or vegetable oils, which are acidic. When the oils are boiled with a strong base (sodium hydroxide) a salt (soap) is formed. Bath salts (sodium carbonate), also used as a soap, are made with carbonic acid.

Even clean drinking water contains many salts, especially those of the metals calcium and magnesium. Some of these salts do not dissolve in water

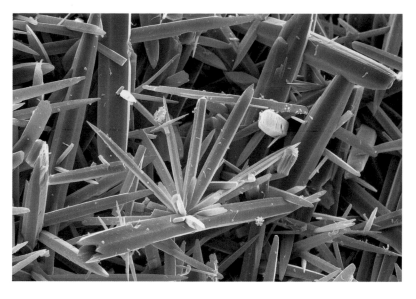

🔴 *Boiling and evaporating water in a kettle leaves behind a layer of salts (shown here greatly magnified). If your water is hard, your kettles, coffee machines, and boilers may "fur up" with these salts.*

but remain as solid impurities. Soap does not lather well in water that contains many salts (called hard water). Instead, it combines with the salts to form a scum, making it less effective at cleaning.

In large amounts the salts in hard drinking water can be bad for us. They can build up and form hard stones in the kidneys and bladder, which can be painful and eventually affect the function of these organs.

You can find out if the water you drink and use for washing is hard or soft (high or low in salts) by conducting the activity on the following pages.

Hydrophilic and hydrophobic

Soap molecules are made up of long chains of carbon and hydrogen atoms. At one end of the chain is a group of atoms that is attracted to water (hydrophilic), and at the other end is a group of atoms that is repelled by water (hydrophobic) but is attracted to grease. When you wash dirty dishes with soap, the hydrophobic end of the soap molecule attaches itself to the grease, letting the water seep in underneath. Grease patches become surrounded by soap molecules, all with their hydrophobic ends pointing inward and their hydrophilic ends pointing out. The hydrophilic ends of the soap molecules then dissolve in the water, and the soap can be washed away, carrying the grease with it. Our bodies make a natural oil that dirt sticks to. The hydrophobic ends of soap molecules also stick to this oil, enabling us to wash away this oil with soap and water.

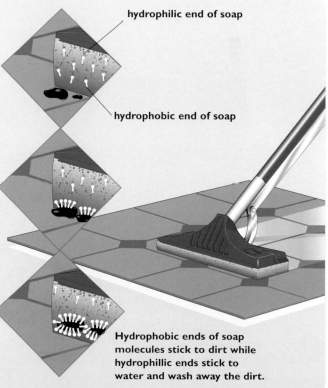

hydrophilic end of soap

hydrophobic end of soap

Hydrophobic ends of soap molecules stick to dirt while hydrophillic ends stick to water and wash away the dirt.

How Hard Is Your Water?

Goals

1. **Find out how hard your water is.**
2. **Learn to compare test results for different quantities.**

What you will need:

- 3 small jars with screw-top lids (baby food jars)
- dishwashing soap
- eyedropper
- distilled water
- water from the faucet
  - salt
  - measuring cup
  - spoon

1 Measure out equal amounts of dishwashing soap and distilled water into the cup. Mix the two to make a solution.

2 Half-fill one jar with water from the faucet. Half-fill the second and third jars with distilled water. Then, add one spoonful of common salt to the third jar.

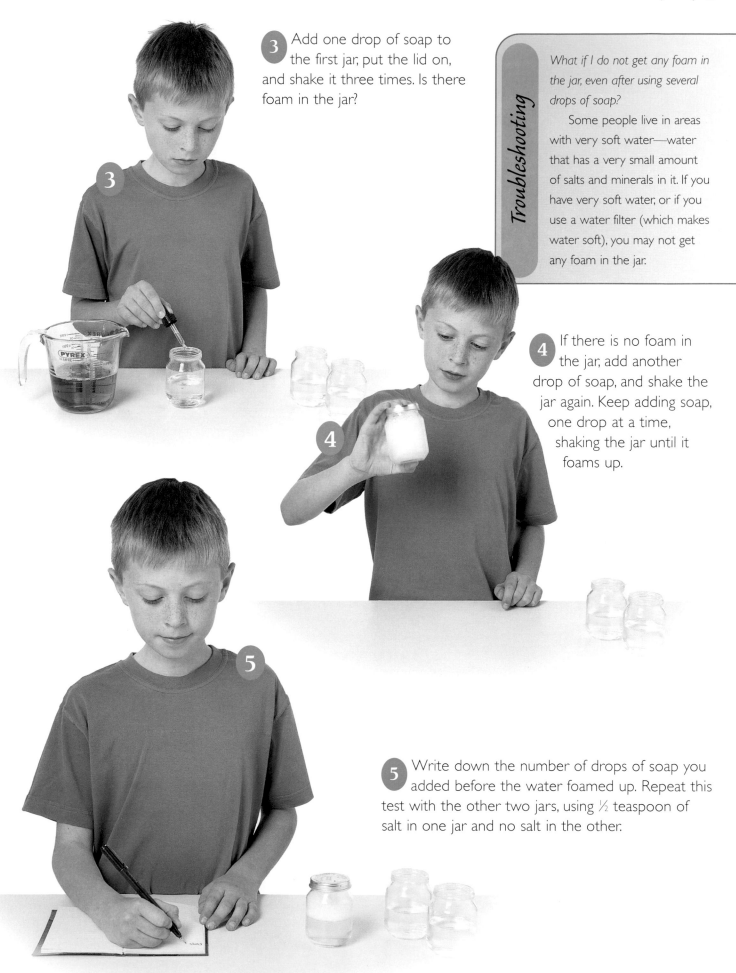

3 Add one drop of soap to the first jar, put the lid on, and shake it three times. Is there foam in the jar?

Troubleshooting

What if I do not get any foam in the jar, even after using several drops of soap?

Some people live in areas with very soft water—water that has a very small amount of salts and minerals in it. If you have very soft water, or if you use a water filter (which makes water soft), you may not get any foam in the jar.

4 If there is no foam in the jar, add another drop of soap, and shake the jar again. Keep adding soap, one drop at a time, shaking the jar until it foams up.

5 Write down the number of drops of soap you added before the water foamed up. Repeat this test with the other two jars, using ½ teaspoon of salt in one jar and no salt in the other.

FOLLOW-UP

How hard is your water?

Water can have varying amounts of salts in it, so it can have varying degrees of hardness. Use the results from your experiment to test faucet water from other places, such as your school, at the playground or park, or at a parent's workplace. Keep a chart of the location where you got the water from and how many drops of soap it took to create a foam. One way to do these tests is to make up a portable water-hardness testing kit. Place a dropper, a small measuring cup, a small jar with a screw-top lid, a second jar with some of your soap mixture in it, your notebook and pencil, and some paper towels in a small box. That is your kit. Use the measuring cup to make sure you always put the same amount of water into your testing jar. When you find some water you would like to test, take your kit out. Place a measured amount of water into the empty jar, perform your test, and write down your results.

Then pour the used water away, and wash the jar and dropper with water, and dry with a paper towel. Pack up your kit, and you are ready for the next test.

■ *You can test a selection of mineral waters for hardness.*

Home
School
Park
Office

Soap added (drops)
1 2 3 4 5

ANALYSIS

Salty soap

In this activity you tested water for hardness by mixing it with soap. When hard water is mixed with soap, it does not lather, but forms a scum instead. The magnesium or calcium atoms in hard water replace the sodium atoms in the soap to make an insoluble scum.

Distilled water is water that has had all the minerals (salts) removed, so you should have found that it only took a few drops of soap solution to form a lather with it. When you added salt to the distilled water, you created hard water. It would have taken a lot more soap solution to make this water lather. The amount of soap solution it takes to make a lather with water from the faucet will depend on the hardness of the water in your area. Water hardness changes dramatically from region to region in a state and may even change from block to block within a city or town. If you performed the follow-up activity and tested water at different locations around your town or city, you would probably have found that the relative hardness of the water was different in different places.

Water that has to be pumped from deep underground is usually harder than water taken from rivers and lakes. That is because water from underground often has the mineral calcium carbonate dissolved in it. This mineral dissolves into the water from the surrounding rock. Regions of the southwestern United States have very hard water for this reason. If you boil some of this very hard water in a kettle or pan until all the water has evaporated, you will see a white, flaky substance left behind. It is the salt calcium carbonate, also called limescale.

Because very hard water can make cleaning difficult, cause "furring up" of faucets, kettles, and water boilers, and even cause health problems, many people who live in hard-water areas use a device called a water softener or ion-exchange column to remove the minerals from the water. Water softeners are usually attached directly to water pipes.

The idea behind a water softener is simple. The calcium and magnesium ions in the salts in the water are replaced with sodium ions. Sodium salts are soluble and do not form a scum with soap. To do the ion exchange, the water in the house is passed through a bed or column containing small plastic beads. The beads are covered with sodium ions. As the water flows past the sodium ions, the calcium and magnesium ions in the salts are replaced by sodium ions. The water that leaves the softener is softer and forms a lather more easily with soap. After some time the beads in the water softener contain only calcium and magnesium ions and no sodium ions. At this point they stop softening the water, and the softening beads must be replaced.

In addition to soap there are several families of salts, each made from a different acid. Sulfates are made from sulfuric acid—plaster of Paris is calcium sulfate. Chlorides can be made industrially using hydrogen chloride gas or hydrochloric acid, although some common chlorides, including table salt (sodium chloride), are extracted from sea water. Carbonates such as bath salts (sodium carbonate) are made with carbonic acid, which is a solution of carbon dioxide gas in water.

Making soap

People have been making soap for thousands of years. Soap is made by heating lye (a strong basic solution) with animal or vegetable fats. Until the 20th century the lye was obtained by filtering water through hardwood ashes. The lye that was trapped was then heated with fatty animal tissue, lard, or oil.

The Romans are often credited with the discovery of soap, around 1000 BC. Legend says that the fat dripping off an animal sacrifice fell into the ashes of a fire. This mixture got into the Tiber River, where women were doing laundry. The women discovered that the clothes were easier to clean with this substance. The soap made at this time was too harsh for the skin and would only have been used for washing clothes. People, such as the African women pictured here, still make soap by hand today. Soapmaking is a cottage industry in many places, only now craftspeople purchase the lye and add colorings, scents, and other materials to the soap.

ACTIVITY 3
BURNING

Combustion (burning) is one of the most common chemical changes. When a substance burns, it combines with oxygen from air, forming new substances and giving off heat and light energy in a violent reaction.

During a chemical reaction the chemical bonds of the reactants (reacting substances) are broken, and some new bonds are formed to create the product molecules. The products usually have different properties from the reactants. Unlike in a physical reaction such as the mixing of sand and water, it is often difficult to reverse a chemical change and get the original substances back.

The breaking of chemical bonds consumes energy, while the forming of chemical bonds releases it. If the production of the new bonds releases more

Fireworks contain explosives that react violently with air when they are lighted (given some initial energy), producing a spectacular exothermic (burning) reaction.

energy than is needed to break the old bonds, then energy is given off during the reaction, usually as heat or light. If the production of the new bonds releases less energy, the energy has to be taken in during the reaction. If the reactants have more energy than the products, then energy has to be taken in during the reaction. Chemical reactions that take

Chemical reactions

In chemical reactions matter and energy are changed from one form to another, but no matter or energy is created or destroyed. For example, when methane (natural gas, like your stove might use) burns in oxygen, new forms of matter (carbon dioxide and water) are formed, and energy is converted from chemical energy inside the reactant molecules to heat and light energy.

Chemical reactions can be described using an equation that involves the chemical formulas and symbols of the reactants and products. The total amounts of energy and matter on both sides of the equation must be the same. In the equation below, methane (CH_4) is heated and reacts with oxygen (O_2) from the air to produce carbon dioxide (CO_2) and water (H_2O).

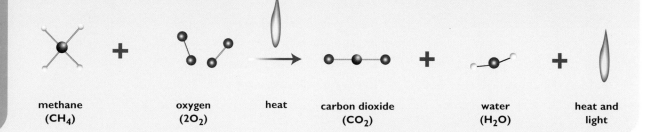

| methane (CH_4) | oxygen ($2O_2$) | heat | carbon dioxide (CO_2) | water (H_2O) | heat and light |

in energy are called "endothermic" reactions (*therm* means "heat," and *endo* means "in"). Energy is taken in as heat energy from the surroundings.

When you put a cold pack on an injury, you are taking advantage of an endothermic reaction. When you bend the cold pack, you break a thin barrier that separates two substances, allowing them to react. An endothermic reaction occurs, and heat energy is taken in from the surroundings—that is, the body part next to the cold pack.

Reactions that give off heat are called "exothermic" reactions (*exo* means "out"). Burning is an exothermic reaction. For example, when wood burns, the reactants (wood and oxygen) have more energy than the products (carbon dioxide, water vapor, and ash). This energy is given off during the reaction in the form of heat and light (as flames).

If burning reactions give off heat, then why do we need to light fires? Most chemical reactions do not start off by themselves—they need an initial "kick" of energy, often in the form of heat, to get going. Even an exothermic reaction such as burning, which gives off a lot of heat, needs a little heat to start the reaction. That is why you need to heat wood a little before it starts burning.

Burning requires oxygen, and many fire extinguishers work by cutting off oxygen from a fire. You can experiment with such an extinguisher here.

Burning wood

Burning (combustion) reactions give off energy in the form of heat. When a substance burns, it combines with oxygen to make a compound called an oxide. Most fuels, such as the wood in the picture below, contain hydrogen and carbon. Hydrogen burns to produce water (as vapor or gas), and carbon burns to form carbon dioxide gas. In enclosed spaces, where not much oxygen is available, carbon burns to form carbon monoxide (which contains less oxygen). Carbon monoxide is poisonous, so fires in closed spaces are dangerous.

Firefighting

Goals

1. **Learn how fire extinguishers work.**
2. **Create and control a reaction.**

- *candle*
- *jar with lid*
- *funnel*
- *plastic tubing, 1 foot (30cm) long*
- *baking soda and vinegar*
- *modeling clay*
- *heatproof dish with sides, like a bowl or a custard dish*
- *tablespoon*

1 Ask an adult to punch a small hole in the lid of the jar. Place the candle into the dish, and ask an adult to light the candle.

2 Insert the tubing into the lid.

3 Seal around the tubing with modeling clay so that there are no gaps between the tubing and the lid.

Safety tip

Be careful around fire. You should ask an adult to supervise the experiment and to light the candle for you. When pointing the tubing at the lighted candle, make sure you do not put the tubing or your fingers too close to the flame.

4 Place about 4 tablespoons of baking soda into the jar.

5 Add about 2 tablespoons of vinegar to the baking soda, and quickly put the lid on the jar.

What if the the flame gets smaller but does not go out?

To produce enough carbon dioxide gas to put the flame out, you may have to use more baking soda and vinegar than the amounts given here. That will depend on the size of your jar, the size of the tubing and funnel, and the size of the candle flame.

6 Point the tubing toward the candle flame. How long does it take the flame to go out?

FOLLOW-UP Firefighting

You can also do this experiment another way. You will need: A short candle, baking soda, vinegar, fire-proof dish, spoon, match, and an adult.

1 Place a short candle in a shallow dish with straight sides. Carefully pack the dish with baking soda all around the candle. Now ask an adult to light the candle for you.

2 Pour vinegar onto the baking soda. What happens? The candle should go out as the carbon dioxide pushes the oxygen away from the wick and the wax, which, in this case, are the fuel for the fire.

ANALYSIS
Burning

Burning is a chemical reaction that can only occur when three things are present: a fuel (something that will burn), oxygen, and heat (there must be enough heat to start the reaction). If you want to put out a fire, you need to remove one of these three things. So, firefighters tackling a forest fire may try to remove fuel by cutting down trees in the path of the fire. They may try to remove heat by putting water on the fire to cool it so that it is not hot enough for the burning reaction to continue. Or they may dump substances on the fire that remove oxygen. In forest fires these substances are usually dropped from aircraft.

Smaller fires in the home can be put out by similar methods. Usually the safest way to put out a fire is by cutting off the oxygen supply. Many fire extinguishers contain carbon dioxide gas, which is heavier than oxygen and pushes it away from the fire. Throwing a fire blanket or damp towel on a fire also cuts off the oxygen supply. You can also use a jet of water to put out some fires, but you must never use water on an electrical fire (you could get a lethal shock) or an oil fire (the burning oil will float on water and may spread more).

Your homemade extinguisher produces carbon dioxide gas that chokes the candle flame. When baking soda and vinegar react together, one of the products of the reaction is carbon dioxide gas. If enough of the gas is produced, it fills up the bottle and flows out of the tube. When you pointed the tube at the candle flame, the carbon dioxide pushed air away from the flame. Without oxygen from the air the candle could not burn, and the flame went out.

ACTIVITY 4
METALS MAKE YOU HEALTHY

Aluminum in lunchboxes and silver in jewelry are metals you can see. But metals are also hidden in other substances—the hemoglobin in your blood cells contains iron, and chlorophyll in green plants contains magnesium.

Most chemical elements are metals, and most metals are hard, shiny substances that conduct heat and electricity well. Some metals, such as iron, cobalt, and nickel, can be made into powerful magnets. Metals can be mixed with other metals or nonmetals to form alloys, such as steel and brass, that have properties similar to metallic elements. Metals can also be chemically combined with other substances, creating compounds that have quite different properties. For example, iron combines with air and water to form soft, dull rust.

TRANSITION METALS

Chemists call metals such as iron, nickel, copper, zinc, silver, and gold "transition metals." Transition metals usually have very high melting points, are particularly hard, and react with nonmetals to form brightly colored compounds. Compounds of iron, such as rust and the hemoglobin in blood cells, are usually red. Many copper compounds are blue or green—notice the color of old copper roofs that have reacted with the atmosphere.

Iron is vital to human life. Hemoglobin in red blood cells contains iron. The iron bonds with oxygen from the lungs and carries it to different parts of the body. Our bodies cannot make iron, so all the iron we need has to come from our food. Leafy green vegetables such as spinach contain a lot of iron. It is important that you get enough iron every day. Some breakfast cereals can provide the iron you need. Many cereal manufacturers add extra iron and other nutrients to make "fortified" cereal. You can remove the iron from cereal and see for yourself that it is the same metal that is used to make nails.

When they are solid, metals form crystals—regularly shaped arrangements of atoms or molecules. Crystals are usually hard and strong. This magnified picture shows the silver crystals in a photographic film.

Iron in Your Breakfast

ACTIVITY

Goals

1. **Separate metal from breakfast cereal.**
2. **Compare the amount of iron in different cereals.**

What you will need:

- *fortified cereal high in iron, such as Total*
- *measuring cup*
- *Ziploc sandwich bags*
- *meat tenderizer*
- *bowl*
- *water*
- *spoon*
- *pencil with an eraser*
- *magnet*
- *small plastic bag*
- *tape*
- *paper towels*

1 Measure out 1 cup of cereal, and pour the cereal into the Ziploc bag. Flatten the bag around the cereal to push the air out, then zip the bag up tightly.

2 Use the meat tenderizer to crush the cereal into a powder.

3 Pour the cereal into a bowl, and add one cup of water. Stir the mixture well.

4 Tape a magnet to the eraser end of a pencil, and seal it inside a plastic bag with tape.

Troubleshooting

What if no iron has stuck to the magnet?

Try repeating the experiment, this time adding more water to the cereal, stirring for longer, and using a stronger magnet. You can also drop the magnet straight into the cereal and stir with a plastic spoon. Then carefully fish the magnet out, and wipe it on a paper towel. You may have to remove pieces of cereal from the paper towel.

5 Stir the cereal with the pencil/magnet for about 10 minutes. (If you are doing this in science class, you could use a magnetic stir bar and stir plate to save your arms the stirring.)

6 Take the magnet out, and wipe the bag it's in with a paper towel. You should see a black, hard powdery substance on the towel. It is the metal iron. In the follow-up you can repeat the experiment with other cereals.

FOLLOW-UP

Iron in your breakfast

Repeat the basic experiment with a selection of different breakfast cereals to find the ones with the most iron.

1 For each cereal measure out a cup of the cereal, and then crush it in a clean Ziploc bag. This is important so that you get more accurate results.

2 Transfer the crushed cereal to a bowl, add one cup of water, and mix thoroughly.

To separate the iron from the cereal, you could use a plastic-coated magnet.

ANALYSIS

Metals make you healthy

You should have been able to remove at least some of the iron from the cereal. In the experiment you used one cup of cereal, equivalent to one serving.

Your body needs iron in the form of ferrous iron—ions of iron that are produced when an iron atom loses two electrons. However, most breakfast cereals contain tiny shavings of iron metal (atoms, not ions). The tiny particles of iron react with hydrochloric acid and other chemicals in the stomach and change into a form that your body can use to make hemoglobin and other essential compounds.

When you mixed the crushed-up cereal with water, you made what chemists call a slurry. A slurry is a mixture of a solid substance and water in which the substance does not dissolve in the water. If you had applied a magnetic field to just the cereal, the force of the magnet would not have been enough to pull the iron particles away from the pieces of cereal to which they are stuck. By crushing the cereal pieces up and mixing with water to form a slurry, you "free" the iron particles from the cereal so that the magnet can attract them.

The iron in some cereals is ground up very finely. In this case you might see what looks like a layer or film of iron on the magnet, rather than small flakes of iron.

It is important to get enough iron in your diet. If you do not eat the right amount of iron, your body cannot produce enough hemoglobin. Your blood will not be able to take up enough oxygen, and you could get a condition called iron-deficiency anemia, which makes you feel tired and weak all the time. Women are more prone to anemia because they lose red blood cells every month during menstruation.

Some women may also become anemic during pregnancy. Children need a lot of iron and are prone to anemia, especially in poor countries, where it is difficult to get enough fresh foods high in iron. Anemia is one of the most common diseases around the world, but it is easy to treat with iron supplements.

Many cereals claim to provide 100 percent of the total daily mineral and vitamin needs in each serving. If you eat cereals that give you 100 percent of your daily needs for iron, you should not take iron supplements, since too much iron can cause problems such as kidney damage. The best solution is to get your iron from potatoes, leafy green vegetables, whole-grain bread, and lean meat, and eat vitamin C (from an orange, for example) at the same meal.

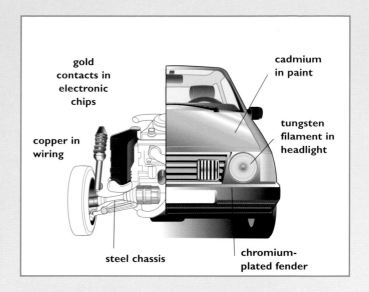

gold contacts in electronic chips

cadmium in paint

copper in wiring

tungsten filament in headlight

steel chassis

chromium-plated fender

■ *This small truck contains various transition metals in the form of elements, alloys, or in compounds. The steel used in the chassis is an example of an alloy of iron.*

Periodic table

The periodic table lists all the elements in order of their atomic number—the number of protons in their atoms. The table is based on one drawn up by the Russian Dimitri Mendeleev (1834–1907) in 1869. Only 63 elements were known then, but Mendeleev left gaps that were filled when new elements were discovered. Elements in the same column (or group) have similar properties. Ninety-two elements occur in nature, and physicists have made more than 20 in laboratories.

atomic number (number of protons in nucleus)

element symbol

6
C
carbon

element name

Legend:
- hydrogen
- alkali metals
- alkaline-earth metals
- transition metals
- lanthanides
- actinides
- noble gases
- nonmetals
- semimetals
- poor metals

1 H hydrogen																	2 He helium
3 Li lithium	4 Be beryllium											5 B boron	6 C carbon	7 N nitrogen	8 O oxygen	9 F fluorine	10 Ne neon
11 Na sodium	12 Mg magnesium											13 Al aluminum	14 Si silicon	15 P phosphorus	16 S sulfur	17 Cl chlorine	18 Ar argon
19 K potassium	20 Ca calcium	21 Sc scandium	22 Ti titanium	23 V vanadium	24 Cr chromium	25 Mn manganese	26 Fe iron	27 Co cobalt	28 Ni nickel	29 Cu copper	30 Zn zinc	31 Ga gallium	32 Ge germanium	33 As arsenic	34 Se selenium	35 Br bromine	36 Kr krypton
37 Rb rubidium	38 Sr strontium	39 Y yttrium	40 Zr zirconium	41 Nb niobium	42 Mo molybdenum	43 Tc technetium	44 Ru rutherium	45 Rh rhodium	46 Pd palladium	47 Ag silver	48 Cd cadmium	49 In indium	50 Sn tin	51 Sb antimony	52 Te tellurium	53 I iodine	54 Xe xenon
55 Cs caesium	56 Ba barium	57-70	71 Lu lutetium	72 Hf hafnium	73 Ta tantalum	74 W tungsten	75 Re rhenium	76 Os osmium	77 Ir iridium	78 Pt platinum	79 Au gold	80 Hg mercury	81 Tl thallium	82 Pb lead	83 Bi bismuth	84 Po polonium	85 At astatine	84 Rn radon
87 Fr francium	88 Ra radium	89-102	103 Lr lawrencium	104 Rf rutherfordium	105 Db dubnium	106 Sg seaborgium	107 Bh bohrium	106 sg seaborgium	109 Mt meitnerium	110 Uun ununnilium	111 Uuu unununium	112 Uub ununbium		114 Uuq ununquadium		116 Uuh ununhexium		118 Uuo ununoctium

| 57 La lanthanum | 58 Ce cerium | 59 Pr praseodymium | 60 Nd neodymium | 61 Pm promethium | 62 Sm samarium | 63 Eu europium | 64 Gd gadolinium | 65 Tb terbium | 66 Dy dysprosium | 67 Ho holmium | 68 Er erbium | 69 Tm thulium | 70 Yb ytterbium |
| 89 Ac actinium | 90 Th thorium | 91 Pa protactinium | 92 U uranium | 93 Np neptunium | 94 Pu plutonium | 95 Am americium | 96 Cm curium | 97 Bk berkelium | 98 Cf californium | 99 Es einsteinium | 100 Fm fermium | 101 Md mendelevium | 102 No nobelium |

ABSORBENT POLYMERS

The plastics that surround you, the fibers in your clothes, and your hair are all made up of long-chain molecules called polymers. Polymers can be hard or flexible, waterproof or absorbent, and have many other properties.

Polymers are long-chain molecules that are made by joining many identical smaller molecules together. The smaller molecules are called monomers. The words "polymer" and "monomer" come from Greek words. *Poly* means "many," *mono* means "one," and *mer* means "part."

Polymers are based on a "backbone" made up of carbon atoms joined together. Of all the elements, only carbon atoms have the unique property of being able to join with other carbon atoms to form chains of almost any length.

Polymers are widespread in nature—sheep's wool consists of polymers, and the tough, fibrous parts of plants are made of the polymer cellulose. Even DNA, the molecule that carries genetic information, and the instructions of life, from generation to generation, is a polymer. The most widespread synthetic materials, plastics, are also polymers.

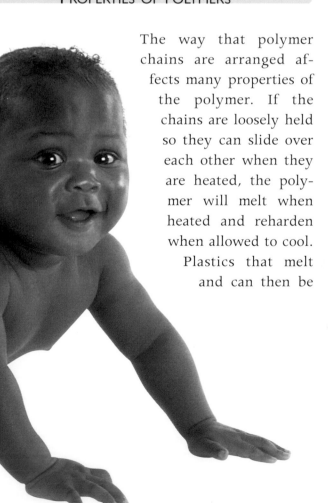

■ *The absorbent material in baby diapers is a polymer that can soak up and hold large amounts of liquids.*

The plastic polyethylene, which is widely used to make bags and sheeting, is based on a monomer called ethylene. Ethylene is made up of two carbon and four hydrogen atoms. The ethylene monomers are linked together by a process called addition polymerization in which the monomers are simply joined together end to end. Some polymers are made by a different method called condensation polymerization, in which each monomer gives up a few atoms to bond with another monomer.

PROPERTIES OF POLYMERS

The way that polymer chains are arranged affects many properties of the polymer. If the chains are loosely held so they can slide over each other when they are heated, the polymer will melt when heated and reharden when allowed to cool. Plastics that melt and can then be remolded are called thermoplastics. Other polymers have chains that are linked together very tightly. These plastics, called thermosets, cannot be re-molded on heating. Plastic chairs are usually made of thermosets.

In living organisms biological polymers are broken down into monomers by enzymes (biological catalysts) so our bodies can use them. In DNA fingerprinting, scientists use enzymes to cut a DNA sample into pieces. The pattern of pieces is unique to the individual supplying the DNA and can be used, like a fingerprint, to identify individuals.

Different polymers have a wide range of different and very useful properties. For example, plastics can be hard enough to make computer cases or flexible enough to make bags or cloth. Different plastics can withstand temperature extremes and corrosive substances. Many polymers are waterproof, but some polymers can absorb a lot of water. These "superabsorbent" polymers are used in disposable diapers. In this activity you will find out how well these polymers absorb liquids, and what happens when they fail.

Diaper polymer

Like all polymers, polyacrylamide, one of the polymers used in diapers, is made of long-chain molecules. The diagram below shows how water becomes attached (bonded) to the polymer. The hydrogen atoms in the polymer have a slightly positive charge. They are attracted to the oxygen atoms in water, which have a negative charge, forming links called hydrogen bonds.

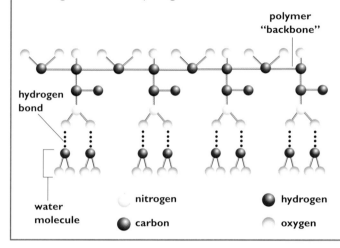

polymer "backbone"

hydrogen bond

water molecule

nitrogen

carbon

hydrogen

oxygen

Absorbing water and salt

The first disposable diapers based on superabsorbent polymers were produced in the 1980s. In these diapers fibers of cotton are mixed with tiny pellets of two superabsorbent polymers: polyacrylate and polyacrylamide. An outer layer of plastic helps prevent leaks. As the diaper becomes wet, the polymers swell and bind the cotton fibers closer together. However, the salt in the baby's urine eventually causes the polymers to begin releasing some of the trapped liquid—that's when the diaper starts to leak, and it's time for a change.

The polymers in diapers are not the most absorbent polymers there are. If more absorbent polymers were used, the diaper would swell up to the size of a bowling ball. You can imagine how uncomfortable that would be!

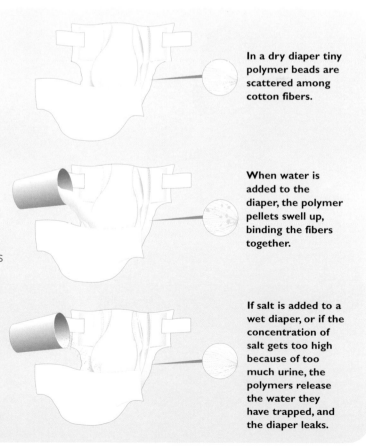

In a dry diaper tiny polymer beads are scattered among cotton fibers.

When water is added to the diaper, the polymer pellets swell up, binding the fibers together.

If salt is added to a wet diaper, or if the concentration of salt gets too high because of too much urine, the polymers release the water they have trapped, and the diaper leaks.

Diaper Science

Goals

1. **Test properties of superabsorbent polymers.**
2. **Find out why diapers can only hold a certain amount of liquid before they have to be changed.**

What you will need:

- unused superabsorbent disposable diapers
- scissors
- twist tie
- large plastic bag
- newspaper
- plastic cup
- measuring cup
- table salt
- spoon

1 First, you have to remove the polymer from the diaper. To do this, cut up a diaper, and put the pieces in a plastic bag.

2 Seal up the plastic bag with a twist tie, grab the neck of the bag, and shake it vigorously for a few minutes. You will notice a white powder coming out of the diaper pieces. Put your hands in the bag, and tease the diaper pieces apart. It may take several minutes to release all the white powder.

3 Open the bag, and remove the plastic cover and all of the shreds of diaper from the bag, and throw them away. Spread newspaper over a table top, and shake the contents of the bag out over the newspaper. You should now be able to scoop up the powder from the newspaper with paper or a spoon. Put half a spoonful in a plastic cup.

Troubleshooting

What if I can't separate the polymer pellets from the diaper?
You can use a pair of tweezers to pick out the individual pellets. If you are still unable to separate the polymer from the diaper, you can purchase the polymer from a garden store in the form of pellets. They are usually advertised as water-absorbing pellets. Ask at your garden store for help in locating them.

4 Add 10 fluid ounces (300ml) of warm water, and stir the two together. What happens?

5 Now add half a teaspoon of table salt to the cup, and stir it in. What changes do you notice?

FOLLOW-UP Diaper science

If you have scientific scales, you can repeat this experiment by weighing out 0.016 ounces (0.5g) of powder instead of using a teaspoon.

To find out the water-holding capacity of the polymer, repeat step 4. This time, after you have added the 10 fluid ounces (300ml) of water, keep adding water, 1½ fluid ounces (50ml) at a time, until the polymer cannot hold any more water. If water spills out when you turn the cup over, the polymer has reached its maximum capacity. You can now calculate how many times its own weight of water the polymer will absorb, using the information that 34 fluid ounces (1,000ml) of water weighs 32 ounces (1,000g). So, if 0.5g of the polymer held 17 fluid ounces (500ml) of water, it absorbed 16 ounces (500g), or 1,000 times its weight of water! You can also measure exactly how much salt it takes to get the polymer to release water by adding the salt in small amounts, such as 0.016 ounces (0.5g) at a time and stirring after each addition of salt.

Try the experiment again using different liquids that are high in salts, such as cola, Gatorade, or another sports drink.

ANALYSIS Absorbent polymers

The white powder in the superabsorbent diapers is made from a mixture of two polymers, polyacrylamide and sodium poly-acrylate. This mixture of polymers can absorb hundreds of times its own weight of water. The monomers in the two substances will break some of their bonds and use these extra bonds to "grab" water molecules and bond to them. You can make the polymers let go of the water molecules by adding salt. Salt is a compound made from sodium and chlorine ions. After a certain amount of salt has been added, the polymer will "drop" the water molecules and bond with the sodium ions instead.

Diaper manufacturers put a small amount of polymer into diapers to make them superabsorbent. As you saw when you took the diaper apart, the manufacturers sandwich the polymer in between layers of fabric, and then cover the fabric with plastic. Urine seeps through the fabric and is absorbed into the polymer. The plastic coating prevents leakage. Because urine is mostly water, the polymer can absorb a lot of urine. But urine also contains sodium. That's why, after a baby has worn a diaper for a while, the diaper begins to leak. Once the level of sodium reaches a certain point, the polymer begins to release the water molecules, and it is time to change the diaper.

There are many other uses for superabsorbent polymers. They are used by farmers for irrigating some crops and also in potting soil for house plants. When you water the plants, the polymers absorb a lot of water, and the plant can then take up this water slowly, over time. That is useful if you are going away on a trip and can't water your plants every day. Superabsorbent polymers are also used to remove water from jet fuel—water is a contaminant that keeps the fuel from burning.

ACTIVITY 6
FERMENTATION

Imagine what meals would be like without bread, cakes, cheese, or yogurt. All of these foods are the result of a chemical reaction called fermentation carried out by tiny microorganisms such as bacteria and yeasts.

Much of the food that we eat undergoes chemical processes before it reaches our plates. For example, bread, cheese, yogurt, wine, and beer are all products of fermentation. Like respiration, fermentation is the conversion of the sugars in food into energy and waste products by an organism. Unlike respiration, fermentation takes place without oxygen. During fermentation microorganisms, such as yeasts, break down the sugars in food, releasing energy. Yeasts in bread, wine, and beer carry out a type of fermentation called alcoholic fermentation. Bacteria in yogurt and cheese are responsible for another type of fermentation called lactic acid fermentation.

Alcoholic fermentation begins when the yeast cell takes up glucose (a type of sugar). Inside the cell the glucose molecule, which contains a chain of carbon atoms, is turned into carbon dioxide and ethanol (a type of alcohol), and energy is released. The energy drives the cell's life processes. Ethanol and carbon dioxide are excreted as waste products.

■ *Cheesemaking is a complex process. Fermentation is carried out by lactic-acid producing bacteria. The cheese is then aged in cellars and may be injected with molds.*

Bread rises because carbon dioxide gas is produced during fermentation. After kneading, the dough is put in a warm place. The yeast breaks down sugars in the flour to make carbon dioxide and ethanol. When you bake bread, the heat kills the yeast and causes the gas trapped in the dough to expand. Unleavened bread, such as pita, is made without yeast and so is flat.

You are probably wondering why bread doesn't make you drunk—after all, ethanol is produced during fermentation. The reason is that when bread is baked, the heat of the oven causes the ethanol to evaporate. Wine and beer are fermented in sealed containers, so the ethanol cannot escape.

Yeast makes carbon dioxide in proportion to the amount of sugar available. You can use this property to compare the sugar content of different foods.

Gas in Bags

Goals

1. **Examine the way yeast breaks down sugar.**
2. **Watch fermentation happen.**
3. **Control the speed of fermentation.**

What you will need:

- 5 large Ziploc bags
- permanent marker pen
- tablespoon
- 2-cup measuring cup
- ¼ cup of sugar
- ¼ cup of flour
- ¼ cup of rice
- 3 cookies
- ¼ cup of juice
- rolling pin
- warm water
- yeast (you can buy cans or packages of bread yeast in any supermarket)

1 Label five Ziploc bags from 1 to 5.

2 Crumble up the cookies until you have ¼ cup. Place the crushed cookies in Bag 1. Next, seal the rice in Bag 2, and crush it by rolling over it with the rolling pin.

Useful bacteria

Yogurt is made by adding certain bacteria, called lactobacilli, to milk and allowing it to ferment. During fermentation the bacteria convert lactose (the main sugar in milk) into lactic acid. The milk becomes thicker as the bacteria multiply. The lactic acid is what makes plain natural yogurt taste sour.

3 Add the following to the numbered bags:
bag 3: ¼ cup sugar
bag 4: ¼ cup flour
bag 5: ¼ cup juice.

4 Add 1 tablespoon of yeast to each bag.

5 Add ¼ cup of warm water to each bag. Squeeze all the air out of the bags, and swirl the contents around to mix them well.

6 Seal all of the bags, and put them in a warm place.

7 After 20 minutes the bags should have swollen up. You can measure the volume of each bag by placing it in the measuring cup and gently pressing the bag in so it fills the cup as much as possible. How much of the measuring cup does each bag fill? The bag that had the most sugar will take up the most room.

Troubleshooting

What if all of my bags swell up an equal amount?

This means that there is too much food sugar in the bags. The yeast is making enough carbon dioxide to fill the bag even from the food that contains least sugar. If this happens, try repeating the experiment using much less of each substance—perhaps just one teaspoonful (and for the cookie, a small chunk.)

Moldy cheese

Cheeses with "holes" or blue "veins" are made by injecting them with molds after the first fermentation stage. A type of penicillin mold gives blue cheese its color and taste. As the cheese ages in the dairy's cellars, small holes are made in it to allow oxygen in for the mold to breathe.

FOLLOW-UP   Gas in bags

There are tastier ways to experiment with fermentation. Many of the foods you eat are made using fermentation. Yogurt and bread are two of them. You can demonstrate fermentation, and have a delicious treat, by making your own bread.

You will need:
1¼ cups warm water
1 tablespoon yeast
½ tablespoon salt
3½ cups unbleached all-purpose flour
mixing bowl
oven
baking sheet
teaspoon
vegetable oil

1 Place the warm water in a mixing bowl. Add the yeast, and stir it with a spoon until it is dissolved. Add the salt and 1½ cups of the flour. Beat the

mixture until the batter is smooth. Slowly add the rest of the flour to make a soft dough (you may need more flour).

2 Knead the dough for about 10 minutes (below), adding more flour if it is very sticky. Add two teaspoons of oil to the dough. Cover the bowl with a

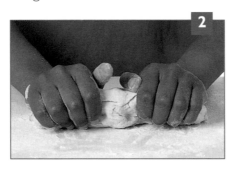

towel, and put it in a warm place for one hour. The dough will rise from the action of the yeast.

3 After an hour push on the dough to squash it down, cover it again, and let it sit for another 30 minutes. Spread a little oil into a loaf pan or onto a cookie sheet. Shape the dough into one large or two small round balls, and place them in the loaf pan, cover, and let them sit for 15 minutes. Turn the oven on at 450 °F (230 °C).

4 Place the loaf on the middle shelf of the oven, and quickly spray water over it to create steam before shutting the oven door. After 5 minutes open the oven, and spray the loaf again. Repeat spraying 2 more times at 10 minutes and 15 minutes. Bake the bread for 25 minutes in total. Ask an adult to remove the bread from the hot oven and cool it on a wire rack.

ANALYSIS
Fermentation

In your original experiment you should have noticed that all the bags swelled up. That is because all of the substances contained sugar. The yeast took in the sugar, broke it down during fermentation, and gave off carbon dioxide gas, making the bags swell. Flour and rice may not taste sweet like sugar or cookies, but they also contain natural sugars that the yeast can use for fermentation. In general, the more sugar, the more the bag will swell up. The yeast also produced liquid ethanol during the fermentation, but you cannot see it in the bags because it is only a small amount and does not separate out as gas does.

▶ *Most of the bread you find in a bakery, apart from pita breads, is leavened. Leavened bread is made by yeast fermentation.*

You may also find that the yeast works better when used with simple sugars that are easy to break down. For example, the sugar in the flour, rice, and cookies is mixed in with many other types of molecules. The yeast will probably work faster in the bag of plain sugar than in these mixtures.

Water was added to the substances in the bags because yeast works best if it is warm and damp. If you wait, eventually the yeast will have used up all the sugar in the substance and the bags will not swell up any more. If you add more sugar, the yeast will get back to work.

In the follow-up you used what you have learned about yeast to make your own bread. Bread rises because the yeast that you added took in the sugar in the flour and gave off carbon dioxide gas. The gas is what makes the bread rise. When you squash down the bread, you are compressing the gas. Then, when you cook the bread, the gas expands (because it gets hotter), pushing the dough up and leaving "holes" (bubbles of gas) in the bread. Without yeast the bread would be flat.

Fermentation and respiration

Yeast is a living microorganism that grows by converting the sugars in foods into carbon dioxide and either ethanol or water. If there is no oxygen present (1), the yeast will make ethanol and carbon dioxide by a process called fermentation. That reaction is used to make alcoholic drinks and bread. If oxygen is present (2), the yeast respires (breathes) rather than ferments. The products of respiration are water and carbon dioxide. Respiration releases more energy than fermentation from the same amount of sugar.

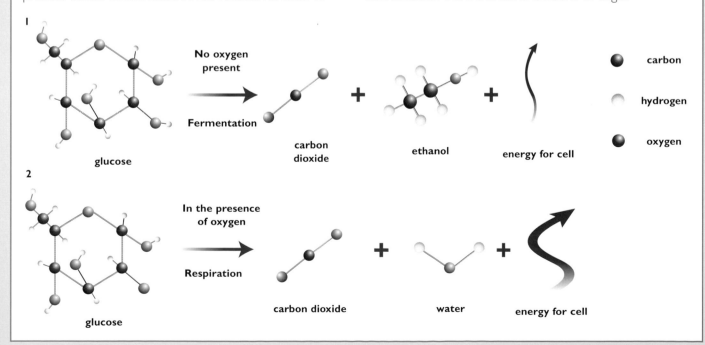

1

glucose → **No oxygen present** **Fermentation** → carbon dioxide + ethanol + energy for cell

2

glucose → **In the presence of oxygen** **Respiration** → carbon dioxide + water + energy for cell

● carbon
○ hydrogen
● oxygen

ACTIVITY 7
CHEMICALS IN FOOD

Like other substances, the foods that we eat can be examined to see what chemicals they contain. There are seven basic types of chemical substances in foods: fats, carbohydrates, proteins, fiber, vitamins, minerals, and water.

We need to get the right amount of nutrients from our food in order to build and repair our bodies and to keep them working properly. Knowing which nutrients are found in different foods helps us stay healthy.

FATS

Fats, also called lipids, are large molecules made up of carbon, hydrogen, and oxygen atoms. They occur in foods such as oil, butter, milk, cheese, nuts, and meat. In the body fats are broken up into smaller molecules that can be transported in the bloodstream and absorbed by cells, either to "burn" as fuel or to be stored for later use. Because they can be stored, fats are a long-term source of energy. Also, certain vitamins dissolve in fats. The only way to get these vitamins is to eat fats that contain them. Your body can make some fats, but others, such as those used to build cell membranes, cannot be made in the body and must be obtained from the foods you eat.

🔲 *We need to eat a variety of different foods to stay healthy. That is because different foods contain different combinations of vital nutrients.*

CARBOHYDRATES

Like fats, carbohydrates are made up of carbon, hydrogen, and oxygen and provide energy. There are two types of carbohydrates—simple carbohydrates, or sugars, and complex carbohydrates, or starches.

The simplest type of sugar is glucose, also called blood sugar because it flows in the bloodstream. Your cells take glucose from blood and "burn" it, releasing energy to drive the cell. Glucose is the body's most basic fuel. Like other sugars, glucose tastes sweet. Fructose is the main sugar in fruits. The liver converts fructose to glucose. Sucrose is white table sugar. Sucrose consists of one glucose and one fructose molecule bonded together.

Starches consist of long chains of glucose molecules. Plants use starches to store energy. Wheat, corn, oats, rice, potatoes, and plantains are high in starch. Your digestive system breaks down starch into smaller glucose molecules that can enter your bloodstream. It takes a lot longer to digest starches than sugars, however. Sucrose, from a can of soda or a candy bar, for example, turns into glucose and enters your bloodstream at the rate of about 30 calories per minute. Complex carbohydrates are digested more slowly, and the glucose enters the bloodstream at a rate of only two calories per minute.

PROTEINS

Proteins are long-chain molecules that contain the elements carbon, hydrogen, oxygen, nitrogen, and sulfur. Each molecule is a chain of smaller units called amino acids. Amino acids provide cells with the building materials that they need to grow and maintain their structure. The digestive system breaks down proteins into amino acids so they can enter the bloodstream. Fish, milk, meat, nuts, and legumes (beans like soybeans) are all rich in protein.

■ *Fiber is found in a variety of plant foods, such as bran, corn, and the wheat in this bread.*

FIBER

Dietary fiber is found mainly in plant foods, such as wheat bran. Fiber is not absorbed by the body—it passes straight through—but it is vital to keep the digestive system healthy.

VITAMINS

Vitamins are small molecules that your body needs to remain healthy. Although humans can make vitamins D and K, the other vitamins must come from food. The human body needs 13 different vitamins: A, B1, B2, B6, B12, C, D, E, K, niacin, folic acid, pantothenic acid, and biotin.

Diseases and disorders can be caused by lack of vitamins. Lack of vitamin C causes scurvy, lack of vitamin K causes internal bleeding, and lack of vitamin A causes night blindness.

Vitamins are found in all fresh foods. Processing foods, for example, by canning, can destroy vitamins, so many processed foods are "fortified"—they have vitamins added to them.

Sunbathing

Vitamin D is present in some foods, but it is also made by the body. In the presence of sunlight the skin converts a type of fat into vitamin D. Exposure to sunlight also causes the skin to make the pigment melanin, which gives skin its color. Melanin absorbs sunlight and produces vitamin D, so darker skin, which has more melanin, also produces more vitamin D.

MINERALS

Minerals are elements that our bodies must get in small quantities from food in order to function properly. Some important minerals are: calcium, needed for teeth and bones; iodine, which is used to make an important hormone; and iron, which is used by red blood cells to transport oxygen.

WATER

You are made up mostly of water—up to 73 percent by weight depending on the amount of fat in your body. Water is vital to life—although we can live for weeks without food, we cannot survive more than a few days without water. You lose about 40 fluid ounces (1.2l) of water a day. Water leaves your body in urine and feces, in your breath when you exhale, and in sweat. This water must be replaced each day from drinks and from food.

You can see what foods contain by using special "testing substances" called reagents that change color in the presence of particular substances.

Testing for Starch and Fat

Goals

1. **Test for starch and fat in different foods.**
2. **Find out if you are eating a healthy diet.**

What you will need:

- ethanol (sometimes sold in hardware stores as methylated spirits)
- 2 measuring cups
- water
- grater
- tablespoon
- strainer
- paper towel
- iodine
- potato
- cookie or other foods to test

1 Grate the potato.

2 Put 1 tablespoon of the grated potato in a cup with ¼ cup of water, and stir.

3 Strain the liquid into another cup.

4 Add a few drops of iodine to the liquid. If the iodine turns a blue-black color, there is starch present.

5 Break up a cookie to make one cup of crumbs.

6 Add ¼ cup of ethanol, and stir.

7 Place a paper towel over the strainer. Strain the liquid into another cup. The liquid should be clear.

8 Add about ¼ cup of water, and stir. If the liquid turns cloudy, fat is present.

FOLLOW-UP Testing for starch and fat

You can use these tests on any foods you want to test. Take a selection of foods, and think about how they taste. Then guess whether or not they have starch or fat in them. Write down your predictions, and then test the foods with your reagents (left). Were your guesses right? Which foods contained both fats and starches?

You can make up a chart of your tests. Label the columns Food, Prediction, Reason for prediction, Reagent used, and Test result.

There are many different types of reagents that you can use to test for other chemicals in food. Your school may already have some of them; or if not, your teacher can order them from a teaching supply store. The following tests are all done in the same way as the iodine test for starch. First, crush up the food. Then add water, and stir. Finally, strain the liquid, and test it with the reagent.

To test for sugar, you can use a reagent called Benedict's solution. If an orange-brown solid mass (precipitate) forms, then sugar is present. To test for vitamin C, you can use a blue solution called DCPIP, which turns colorless in the presence of vitamin C.

To test for protein, add dilute sodium hydroxide solution and a few drops of pale blue copper sulfate solution to the food. The solution will change color to pale purple if there is protein present in the food.

ANALYSIS Chemicals in food

In the activity you used some basic reactions of starches and fats to see if they were present in different foods.

In the starch test the iodine reacted with the starch to make a new compound. This compound is blue-black in color. If there is no starch present, then the blue-black compound is not made, and the iodine remains orange.

Fats do not dissolve in water, but they do dissolve in alcohol. Adding ethanol (a type of alcohol) to crushed-up food in the fat test will cause any fats that might be in the food to dissolve, making a clear solution. You filtered the solution to remove any undissolved food, leaving just the ethanol and any dissolved fats. Ethanol dissolves in water, but fats do not. So when you mixed the ethanol containing dissolved fats with water, the ethanol mixed well with the water, but the fats dissolved in the ethanol did not mix. That caused the liquid to become cloudy. If there were no fats present, the mixture would have remained clear.

Another test for fats is to rub the food you want to test onto a paper towel. If the towel becomes damp and then later dries out, the food contains water. If a greasy patch that doesn't dry out forms on the towel, the food is fatty.

Cooking changes food chemically. For example, some protein molecules are joined together in long chains. When you cook protein—for example, when you fry an egg—the protein molecules first unravel and then tangle up together to form a solid mesh. That is why runny egg whites and yolks become solid when they are cooked. Cooks use this chemical reaction when they add eggs to dishes in order to bind food together (make it solid).

Fats, such as butter and oil, will easily combine with sugar molecules to trap air. That's one reason why cooks add butter to cakes. The butter and sugar are whipped together to trap air. When the cake mixture is cooked in a hot oven, the trapped air expands (gases expand when they are heated), making the cake "rise" and become soft and fluffy.

It is important to remember that the key to a healthy diet is to eat a balanced amount of all the vital nutrients. It is okay to eat a little sugar, for example, but too much can cause dental and other problems. The more you know about what you eat, the easier it will be for you to choose foods that will keep you healthy.

Food pyramid

This food pyramid is an easy way to remember what kinds of foods you should be eating a lot of, and what kinds of foods you should be eating only in moderation in order to remain healthy. You should eat more of the foods at the bottom of the pyramid. One serving is equal to 4 ounces (100 grams).

At the top of the pyramid are oils and solid fats like butter, and sugar. You should only eat a small amount of these things. Lower down on the pyramid are milk, yogurt, cheese, fish, meat, poultry, eggs, and nuts. You should eat two to three servings (8-12 ounces, or 200–300 grams) of these

foods every day. Below these groups are fruits and vegetables. Eat between two and five servings (8-20 ounces, or 200-500 grams) of them every day. They make great snacks. At the base of the pyramid are the foods that should be the base of your diet—carbohydrates such as bread, rice, pasta, and cereals. You should eat between six and eleven servings (24-44 ounces, or 600-1100 grams) of these foods every day. Eating whole-wheat foods like bran, brown rice, and bread made with whole-wheat flour, will provide you with fiber, which is necessary for keeping your bowels and intestines working properly.

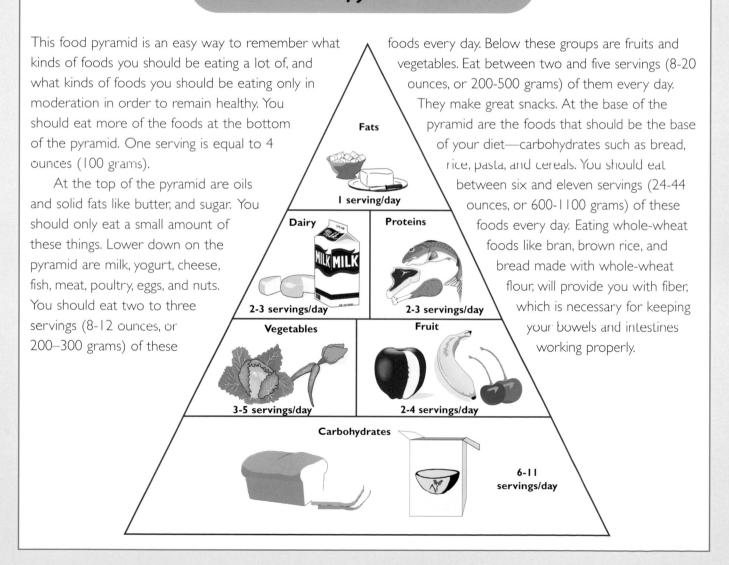

Fats
1 serving/day

Dairy
2-3 servings/day

Proteins
2-3 servings/day

Vegetables
3-5 servings/day

Fruit
2-4 servings/day

Carbohydrates
6-11 servings/day

ACTIVITY 8
MILK MAKES ME SICK

To digest food and process it for use by your body, you need proteins called enzymes. Digestion involves many enzymes, each doing a specific job. If milk makes you sick, you don't have the right enzyme to digest it.

Some chemical reactions happen whenever two substances come together. For example, whenever some atoms of potassium and molecules of water meet, a very fast chemical reaction occurs. The potassium reacts violently with water, producing potassium hydroxide and hydrogen gas, which burns. We describe this by saying that potassium is highly reactive with oxygen. However, for some other chemical reactions to take place at all or to speed up a chemical reaction, an additional substance called a catalyst is needed. Unlike the reactants (starting substances), catalysts are not used up at all during the reaction.

Like human milk, cow's milk contains lactose. People with lactose intolerance are unable to drink cow's milk. One solution is to drink lactose-free soy milk.

Catalysts speed up reactions by reducing the amount of energy needed for the reaction to happen. Many catalysts act as a bridge between the reactants in a reaction, bringing the molecules close enough to react. At the end of the reaction the catalyst can be recovered unchanged. Living things use catalysts called enzymes. Without enzymes the chemical reactions inside our bodies would need more energy to occur than we could ever take in.

You can see enzymes at work in the digestion of milk. Human (and cow's) milk contains a complex sugar, or carbohydrate, called lactose. Lactose is made up of two simple sugars, called glucose and galactose, bonded together. In Activity 7: Chemicals in Food you learned that our bodies use simple sugars for energy. Complex sugars, such as lactose, first have to be broken down into simple sugars by our bodies before they can be digested. That takes a lot of energy. To get around this problem, our bodies use an enzyme called lactase to help break up the lactose into the simple sugars galactose and glucose.

Most human babies make a lot of lactase—after all their only food is milk. But once babies start eating solid foods, their bodies begin to make less and less lactase. Some adults do not make any lactase at all, and so they cannot break down the lactose in milk and milk products. This condition is called lactose intolerance. People with lactose intolerance feel bloated and full, and often have diarrhea and stomach cramps, after drinking milk or eating foods made with milk. However, they can drink lactose-free soy milk or use lactase drops.

Catalysts in cars

Fuel cells use a metal catalyst—often platinum—to cause a reaction between hydrogen and oxygen that produces water. This reaction also generates electricity, which can be used to power vehicles (see photo below). Because fuel cells give off only water, they are a very clean form of energy. It is hoped that someday all vehicles will use fuel cells for power.

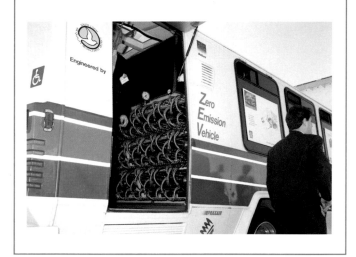

Catalysts and enzymes

Catalysts are substances that speed up chemical reactions. Catalysts called enzymes speed up chemical reactions in living things and make life possible. Enzymes work by lowering the amount of energy needed for reactions to take place. Without enzymes the chemical reactions that take place in cells would take more energy than living things have available in their bodies. There are hundreds of thousands of different enzymes.

The enzyme shown below is maltase. Maltase is shaped to accept a maltose molecule; it will not accept any other molecule. Maltose is a complex sugar, similar to lactose, that is made up of many glucose molecules bonded together. Our bodies cannot use maltose because it is too large, so the maltase breaks the maltose up into glucose, which our bodies can use. A single maltase enzyme can break over 1,000 maltose bonds each second.

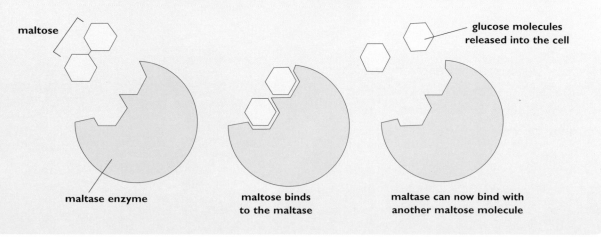

maltose

glucose molecules
released into the cell

maltase enzyme

maltose binds
to the maltase

maltase can now bind with
another maltose molecule

Enzymes in Action

Goals

1. **Examine how enzymes work to break down molecules.**
2. **Discover how to break down molecules.**
3. **Study the causes of lactose intolerance.**

What you will need:

- water
- beaker or glass
- regular milk
- nonfat milk
- lactose-free milk, such as soy or rice milk
- lactase drops (available in most drugstores)
- plastic cups
- glucose test strips (available in drug stores)
- glucose (available as a powder or tablets in drugstores) and tablespoon

1 Pour ½ cup of water into a beaker or glass. Add a tablespoon of glucose, and stir well to make a solution.

2 Dip a glucose test strip into the solution. Compare the color change on the strip to the key on the package to find out the amount of glucose in the solution. Write it down.

3 Now fill a plastic cup with nonfat milk, and repeat the test with the test strip, recording your results.

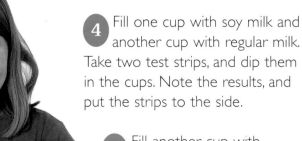

4 Fill one cup with soy milk and another cup with regular milk. Take two test strips, and dip them in the cups. Note the results, and put the strips to the side.

5 Fill another cup with regular milk. Add a few lactase drops to the milk in this glass, and then test it like the others.

6 Compare the colors of all the test strips to determine the amount of glucose in all four cups. Which has the most glucose? Which contains the least amount?

Nonenzyme catalysts

Methanol is a clear liquid that can be stored in a bottle for a hundred years without changing. But if it passes over a heated catalyst called a zeolite, it immediately undergoes a chemical reaction and turns into gasoline. This reaction is now used in New Zealand as part of an industrial process for converting natural gas into gasoline.

Troubleshooting

What if the glucose test strip doesn't change color?

There are several different types of glucose test strip. Most of them are designed to test the amount of glucose in blood. The ones designed to test for glucose levels in urine work best here.

FOLLOW-UP

Enzymes in action

Test the amount of lactose in other milk products, such as yogurt, butter, and cheese, before and after adding lactase drops. You will have to melt the butter and cheese first. You can do that in a microwave or on the stove—but make sure you ask an adult to help.

You can also try changing the temperature of the milk and other liquids by heating them gently. Does this have any effect on the amount of glucose that they contain?

You can also test nonmilk products for glucose, such as orange juice or other types of juice. Which ones contain the most glucose?

A large number of of people in the world are lactose intolerant as adults. Lactose intolerance is especially common among Native Americans and Asian-Americans. Take a survey of the parents of your class members. Find out where their family came from originally, and if they are lactose intolerant.

■ *You can test for the presence of glucose in melted cheese or butter. Add some drops of lactase to the substance, and test again.*

ANALYSIS

Milk makes me sick

The lactase enzyme breaks down milk sugar into glucose and galactose, making it digestible for people with lactose intolerance.

Regular milk contains a high concentration of lactose and no glucose, so it should not turn the glucose test strip any color. The lactose-free milk has already been treated with lactase. When you tested the lactose-free milk, the glucose strip should have changed color, indicating the presence of glucose.

After you added lactase drops to the regular milk, the lactose was broken down, and the glucose strip should have changed color to indicate the presence of glucose.

In yogurt bacteria break down some of the lactose naturally, so the test strip should have shown the presence of some glucose before you added the enzyme drops, but much more glucose after you added the drops.

Bacteria also break down lactose in cheese. Some people who are lactose intolerant can often eat cheese and yogurt, because in these foods bacteria has done the work of lactase.

Enzymes act faster when they are warm, so if you heated the milk in the follow-up, you may have noticed more glucose present after the lactase was added: More of the lactose was broken down because of the heat.

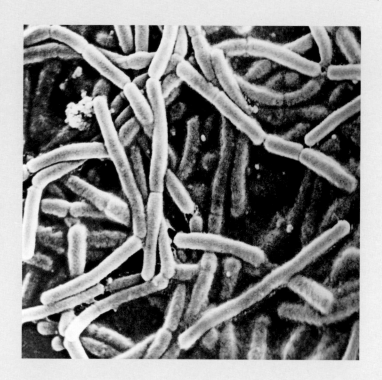

If you did the survey suggested in the follow-up, you may have found that the people who can digest milk (are lactose tolerant) had ancestors who came from cultures where people drank a lot of milk or milk products throughout their lives. In particular, people whose livelihood depends on milk-producing animals, such as dairy cows, sheep, and goats, usually drink a lot of milk.

In some parts of the world people did not commonly raise milk-producing animals until relatively recent times. These people would not have drunk milk after they were babies. Their bodies stopped wasting energy making lactase that they weren't using. Many of the people whose ancestors came from areas where milk-producing animals were scarce are lactose intolerant. In particular, Native Americans, Inuits, Pacific Islanders, and people from some parts of Southeast Asia, such as Korea and Japan, are often lactose intolerant.

■ *Lactobacilus (above) are the bacteria that turn milk into into yogurt and cheese. They break down lactose into simple sugars, doing the work of enzymes.*

Louis Pasteur

Although milk is an important part of our diet, it was not always safe to drink. Until fairly recently milk was a source of many diseases, including tuberculosis. The germs that cause these diseases found a perfect breeding ground in raw milk, which contains sugars. In the past many people died each year from diseases caused by milk-borne bacteria. Today the milk that you buy in the store has been pasteurized to kill any harmful bacteria. Pasteurization was developed by French chemist and microbiologist Louis Pasteur (1822–1895), who also developed the germ theory of disease.

High heat kills bacteria, but it also destroys nutrients. In the pasteurization process milk is heated to 160 °F (70 °C) for 15 seconds and then cooled quickly. This preserves the flavor and most of the nutrients in the milk while destroying any bacteria. Milk can be preserved for longer by killing even more of the bacteria by radiation or very high temperatures, but these processes affect the nutrient content or taste.

ACTIVITY 9
PIGMENTS

Plant and animal life on Earth comes in a dazzling range of colors—think of red, green, and yellow vegetables, multicolored parrots, and color-changing chameleons. These colors are caused by substances called pigments.

Open up your refrigerator, and take a look at the vegetables inside. You might see orange carrots, red cabbage, tomatoes, or beets, green onions, leeks, or lettuce, and so on. These various colors are all due to large molecules inside the vegetables called pigments. The colors of carrots and tomatoes are caused by pigments called carotenoids. Spinach and other green vegetables get their color from the pigment chlorophyll. Other colors are caused by combinations of different pigments.

Besides chlorophyll there are three other types of plant pigments. Carotenoid pigments (such as beta carotene, found in orange carrots) are responsible for orange, red, and brownish colors. The anthocyanins make purple, blue, black, and red colors.

Anthoxanthins make orange, yellow, and white colors. As you have probably realized, many plants contain more than one pigment. Different pigments combine to make a mixture of colors, or the color of one pigment masks the color of the others.

Pigment molecules reflect certain wavelengths (or colors) of light and absorb other wavelengths. For example, when white light (a mixture of all the colors of light) shines onto chlorophyll, only light in the green part of the spectrum is reflected back into our eyes, so we see the color green.

◗ *Plants and algae, like this seaweed, that contain the green pigment chlorophyll are capable of producing their own food, using energy from sunlight.*

But pigments in plants serve important functions other than just giving the plant color. They also help manufacture important substances that plants, and the animals that feed on them, need. For example, beta carotene (found in orange carrots) can be changed into vitamin A, which is needed for good eyesight in humans and other animals.

You may already know that in the presence of sunlight, chlorophyll allows plants and algae to produce food. Most plants and algae contain chlorophyll, even if they are not green. In some the color of the chlorophyll is hidden by other pigments. For example, brown seaweed contains chlorophyll and a carotenoid pigment that gives the seaweed its color. Underwater the only light available is greenish, which chlorophyll cannot absorb. The red pigment absorbs the energy of the green light and passes it on to the chlorophyll.

Human skin contains the pigment melanin. The more melanin in the skin, the darker the skin color. If you get a suntan, your skin produces more melanin.

Animal color

Animals have pigments in their skin, fur, or feathers. These colors serve various functions—the most important being camouflage, or disguise. Animals use their camouflage to hide from predators, to attract a mate, or when hunting for prey. Some butterflies and other insects have camouflaged themselves by resembling sticks or leaves. Others mimic the coloring of poisonous creatures. Many male birds have vibrantly colored feathers that they display to attract females. Chameleons can change their skin color by changing the size and shape of cells containing different pigments. This gives the chameleon (see picture, right) the ultimate camouflage as it lies in wait for its insect prey. Cuttlefish and octopi can also change color to match their surroundings or to communicate.

Humans also have pigments in their skin—just look around your class at school. The variety of different skin tones is caused by different amounts of the pigment melanin. The more melanin, the darker the skin.

Color-coded Vegetables

Goals

1. **Discover which pigments are found in different vegetables.**

2. **Practice methods of extracting pigments from vegetables.**

What you will need:

- *carrots and other brightly colored vegetables*
- *melted butter*
- *tissue paper or blotting paper*
- *grater*
- *measuring cylinder or teaspoon and tablespoon*
- *cutting board*
- *jars or glasses*
- *mineral oil*
- *strainer or funnel*

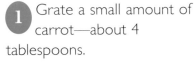

1 Grate a small amount of carrot—about 4 tablespoons.

2 Put half the grated carrot in a cup, and mix it with two teaspoons of mineral oil.

3 Place the strainer or funnel over the mouth of a jar, and line it with tissue paper. Pour half the carrot-mineral oil mixture through the tissue paper. After a few minutes a solution containing the pigment will have dripped through. Set it aside.

4 Mix the other half of the grated carrot with one teaspoon melted butter and 2 teaspoons of mineral oil.

5 Place the funnel or strainer lined with tissue over a second jar, and pour in the carrot-mineral oil-butter mixture. After a few minutes the pigment solution will have dripped through. Set this solution aside.

6 Hold the jars up to a light, and compare the colors of the first and second solutions. Repeat the activity with different vegetables.

Squid ink

Squid and their cousins, cuttlefish, escape from their predators by squirting a cloud of black ink into their path. The pigment in cuttlefish ink, called sepia, was used in the 19th century to give photographs a brown tint. Today synthetic pigments are used in photography, but squid's ink is still used to give some pasta a black color.

FOLLOW-UP

Color-coded vegetables

You can test a variety of brightly colored vegetables using this method. Tomatoes and spinach are good vegetables to use. Or, you can try the following experiment to separate the different pigments in lettuce.

For this experiment you will need: radicchio lettuce (or another red lettuce), acetone (nail polish remover), a blender, glass bowl, blotting paper (or tissue paper), cotton swabs, a glass, and a strainer.

In this activity make sure you do not breathe in the acetone or get it near your mouth or nose. Do not put acetone in a plastic cup or plastic blender, since it will dissolve the plastic.

1 Take the red tops of two or three radicchio lettuce leaves, and blend them until they are mushy. Put the mush in the glass bowl with an equal

amount of nail-polish remover. Strain the mush into another bowl. You should have a colored liquid in the bowl. Cut the blotting paper into strips about 2 inches (5cm) by 10 inches (25cm). Draw a line about 1 inch (2.5cm) from the bottom of each strip in pencil. Arrange a piece of blotting paper upright in the glass.

2 Cut the end off a cotton swab. Dip the cut end into the liquid, and touch it to the blotting paper in the middle of the line you have drawn. Wait for the spot to dry, and repeat this two or three times.

3 Mix ¼ cup of acetone with ¼ cup of water, and add 3 tablespoons of this solution to the glass. Leave for about 10 minutes, until the liquid has soaked most of the way up the blotting paper. Let the paper dry. What do you see?

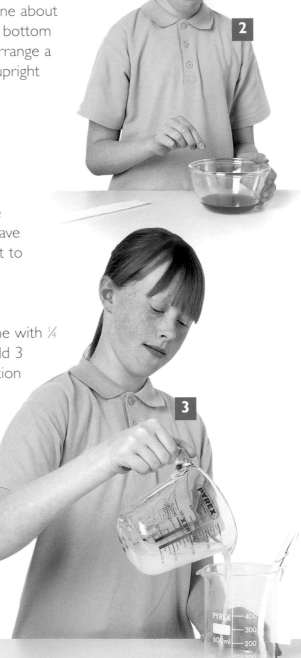

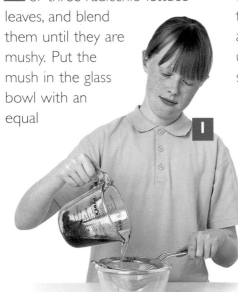

ANALYSIS

Pigments

Many pigments, such as beta carotene (an orange pigment) and chlorophyll (a green pigment) are fat soluble. This means that they dissolve in fats, like oil and butter. In the activity you used two different kinds of fat to extract as much pigment as possible from the plants. You would only have been able to extract fat-soluble pigments in this experiment. Since not all pigments are fat soluble, you may not have been able to remove all of the pigment from each type of vegetable that you tried. Which ones contained fat-soluble pigments? The vitamins that are contained in pigments are also fat soluble. Your body cannot absorb these vitamins unless they are dissolved in fats—that is one of the reasons why it is important to have enough fats in your diet.

In the follow-up activity you used acetone instead of fat to dissolve the pigment. Acetone will dissolve some pigments that are not soluble in fat. If you did the follow-up experiment, you would have noticed that the colored spots at the bottom of the paper separated into different colors farther up the paper. The acetone separated the pigments and carried them up the paper, enabling you to see them more easily. The colors separated out because molecules of different pigments have different weights and are carried by the acetone at different speeds. Red lettuce leaves contain both chlorophyll and red-brown pigments, so you should have seen two separate spots on your paper: a green spot and a reddish-brown spot.

The red pigment in lettuce is there to protect the plant from too much sunlight. If there is too much light, the chlorophyll absorbs energy faster than the plant can use it. This extra energy is bad for the plant. The red pigment absorbs some of the extra energy from the Sun to protect the plant.

Vegetables

Different fruits and vegetables contain different pigments. Some pigments help the plant capture and use light. Other pigments help fruits and flowers stand out from the surroundings so insects and birds that help pollinate the plants or spread seeds are attracted to them. Some pigments are associated with different vitamins. That is one reason why we need to eat a variety of different fruits and vegetables. For example, carrots contain the pigment beta carotene (from which vitamin A is made). The next time you are in a supermarket, see how many different colors of fruits and vegetables you can find.

ACTIVITY 10
FRUITY DNA

How does a caterpillar become a butterfly? Why does a zebra have stripes? Why do we look like our parents? Because of DNA. DNA carries the "instructions for life" for all living things.

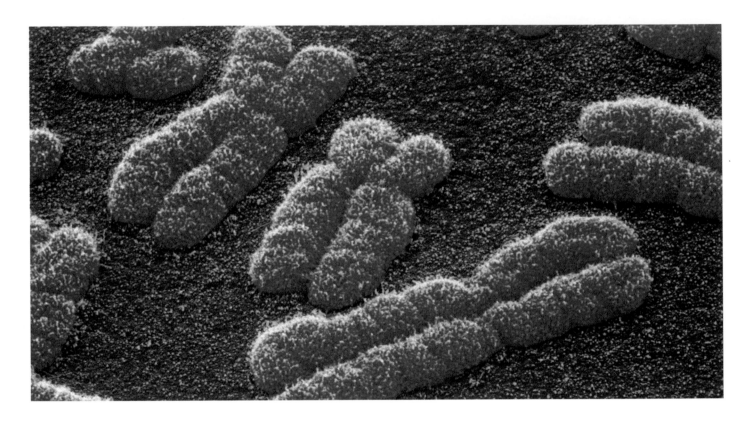

🔴 *Strands of DNA coil up to make chromosomes. Here the chromosomes have duplicated themselves, ready to split when the cell duplicates itself.*

Every cell in your body contains DNA (deoxyribonucleic acid)—a long molecule that carries instructions for making the proteins that your cells need. DNA consists of two long strands that wind around each other like a ladder in a shape called a double helix. Each strand has a "backbone" made of a sugar called deoxyribose and a substance called phosphate. Each backbone carries a long sequence of bases—four substances called adenine (A), cytosine (C), guanine (G), and thymine (T), which carry the actual information for life. A typical DNA molecule may have several millions of these bases.

The bases are arranged along the two strands. Bases on each strand pair up, forming weak bonds between the two strands. Bases A and T always pair up, as do C and G. The arrangement of the bases along the DNA molecule "spells" out instructions that are decoded by other molecules. For example, "AGGTCTGACGCT" might tell the cell to make a small part of a protein that helps digest food.

DNA occurs in all living things, from bacteria to redwood trees to polar bears. In humans the DNA in each cell is spread across 23 pairs of chromosomes—microscopic structures containing coiled-up DNA. Groups of bases along DNA carry particular instructions that are called genes. Genes occur in pairs (one on each strand of a length of DNA). We inherit one gene of each pair from each of our parents—that is what makes us look a little like each parent. Some genes carry "bad" information, and sometimes genes can become damaged. Such genes are involved in causing certain diseases. Our genes, the cnvironment in which we live, and our diets and lifestyles all work together to determine how healthy we are.

The structure of DNA was worked out in 1953 by Francis Crick (born 1916) and James Watson (born 1928). Watson and Crick first had to remove the DNA from a cell so that they could study its structure. You can duplicate the methods used in their early experiments yourself by extracting the DNA from fruit.

Francis Crick and James Watson.

DNA

Animal and plant cells contain a control center called the nucleus. Packed inside the nucleus are huge molecules of deoxyribonucleic acid (DNA). The DNA molecules are shaped a little like twisted ladders. This shape is called a double helix. The sides of the ladder are made of a sugar called deoxyribose and another molecule called a phosphate group. The rungs of the ladder are made of four bases, linked in pairs: adenine, cytosine, guanine, and thymine. Inside the nucleus the large DNA molecules form structures called chromosomes. The chromosomes contain the instructions that control the processes of the cell.

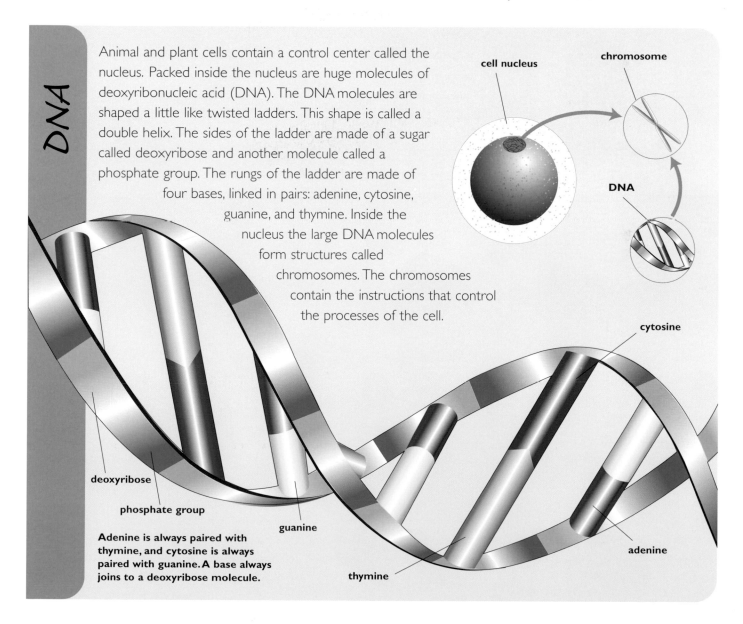

Adenine is always paired with thymine, and cytosine is always paired with guanine. A base always joins to a deoxyribose molecule.

Extracting DNA

Goals

1. **Separate DNA from fruit cells.**
2. **Observe and extract DNA from a mixture.**

What you will need:

- large bowl of ice
- bottle of methylated spirits
- kiwi fruit
- knife and chopping board
- 2 measuring cups
- kitchen scales
- table salt
- measuring cylinder
- dishwashing liquid (not concentrated)
- water
- large saucepan of hot water
- strainer
- large spoon
- champagne flute or other tall, thin glass
- a piece of bare wire

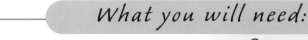

1 Place the bottle of methylated spirits in the ice. The spirits must be very cold.

2 Peel the kiwi fruit, and cut it into small pieces on the chopping board. Put the pieces in the measuring cup.

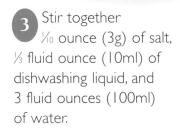

3 Stir together ¹⁄₁₀ ounce (3g) of salt, ⅓ fluid ounce (10ml) of dishwashing liquid, and 3 fluid ounces (100ml) of water.

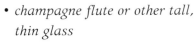

4 Add the dishwashing liquid–salt solution to the chopped-up fruit in the measuring cup, and let it sit for 15 minutes.

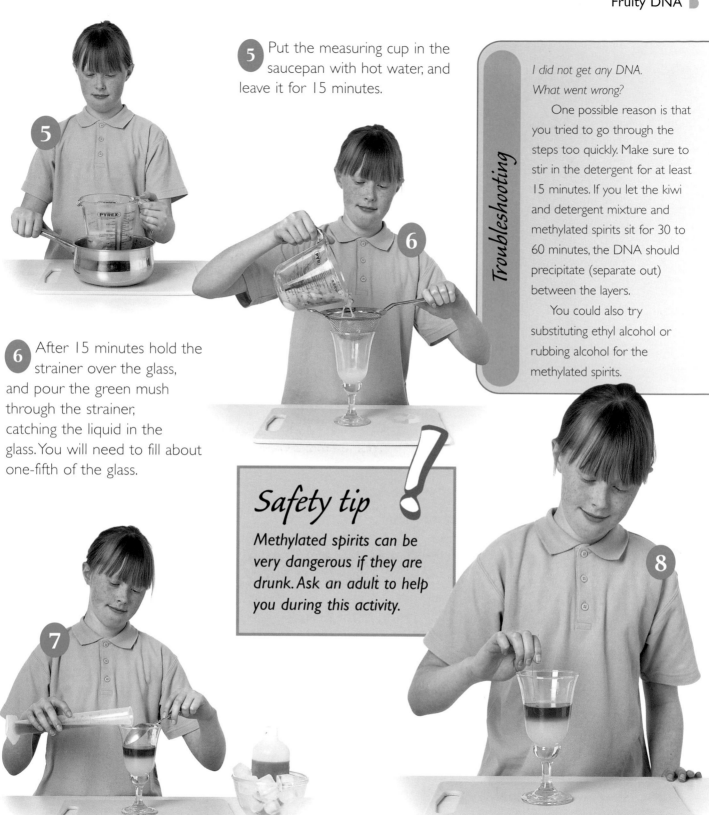

5 Put the measuring cup in the saucepan with hot water, and leave it for 15 minutes.

Troubleshooting

I did not get any DNA. What went wrong?

One possible reason is that you tried to go through the steps too quickly. Make sure to stir in the detergent for at least 15 minutes. If you let the kiwi and detergent mixture and methylated spirits sit for 30 to 60 minutes, the DNA should precipitate (separate out) between the layers.

You could also try substituting ethyl alcohol or rubbing alcohol for the methylated spirits.

6 After 15 minutes hold the strainer over the glass, and pour the green mush through the strainer, catching the liquid in the glass. You will need to fill about one-fifth of the glass.

Safety tip

Methylated spirits can be very dangerous if they are drunk. Ask an adult to help you during this activity.

7 Very carefully drizzle the ice-cold methylated spirits on the back of spoon so that it forms a purple layer on top of the green layer. Stop when the glass is about two-fifths full. Set the glass on the table, and watch.

8 You should see a white layer form in between the green and purple liquids. It is DNA. Fish the DNA out by winding it carefully on the wire.

FOLLOW-UP

Extracting DNA

You can examine your kiwi DNA under a microscope, but you would need an extremely powerful microscope to see the base pairs and the structure of DNA. These microscopes are large and expensive, and are used mostly in research labs.

You can also remove the DNA from different foods (right), using the same technique. Raspberries, green split peas, and wheat germ work very well. If you are using food that is hard to chop up, blend the food in a blender together with an equal amount of water and a pinch of salt. After the food is blended, strain it into a bowl or measuring cup, add detergent, and let the mixture sit for 15 minutes. Then continue the experiment as before.

Compare the amounts of DNA that you can remove from different foods. Is it always about the same amount of DNA? You might think that fruit cells would have less DNA than human cells, but actually they contain about the same amount.

ANALYSIS

Fruity DNA

DNA occurs in every cell of every living thing, but the tricky part is to get it out of the cell without damaging it. There are really two problems: You have to get the DNA out of the cell, and you also have to separate the DNA from the proteins that are inside every cell.

The first problem is solved by chopping up the kiwi fruit and letting it soak in detergent and salt. The detergent and salt strip away the cell membranes (proteins that surround the cell and hold the contents of the cell in) and let all the cell contents escape. The finer you chop your kiwi, the more cells are broken open. But if you overdo it by putting your kiwi in a blender, you may smash the DNA as well. The blender works well with some foods, however.

The second problem, getting rid of the protein that sticks to the DNA inside the cell, is partly solved for you by the kiwi fruit and partly by the methylated spirits. Kiwi fruit contains a lot of enzymes called proteinases. A proteinase's job is to dissolve proteins. The proteinase enzyme attacks the proteins that cling to the DNA and breaks them up, releasing the DNA. That's why kiwi fruit works well for this experiment: The "chopping-up" enzymes exist naturally in the kiwi fruit.

The green layer in your glass is full of DNA as well as lots of broken-up proteins and a lot of other stuff from inside the cell. When you pour the cold methylated spirits into the glass, the DNA dissolved in the green layer turns into

Although Crick, Watson, and Maurice Wilkins (born 1916) shared the Nobel Prize in Physiology or Medicine in 1962, it was Rosalind Franklin (1920–1958) who took and analyzed the X-ray photos of DNA crystals that showed Crick and Watson the structure of DNA. Franklin died before her work could be rewarded.

a solid. This solid then rises to the top of the green layer and shows up as the white layer, at which point you can fish it out.

Each cell of your body contains about 6 feet (20m) of DNA, stretched out. Since there are around three trillion cells in your body, that means that if all the DNA in your body was un-wound and stretched out, it would measure about 3.5 million miles (5.6 million km). And yet each strand of DNA is only 10 or 12 atoms wide, so it can coil together tightly to fit into the small space inside your cells.

Dissolving ions

Every strand of DNA contains a code, like the code in a computer, that tells the cells what to do. The code is the order of the bases. A sequence of three bases, such as AGT, gives the code for a particular amino acid—the building blocks of proteins. So several such sequences will give the complete instructions for building a protein. There are 3 billion pairs of bases in human DNA.

One of the techniques that scientists have for deciphering the DNA code is called gel electrophoresis (right). In gel electrophoresis pieces of DNA are placed in a gel, and electricity is passed through it. The DNA fragments, which carry small electrical charges, move through the gel because of the electricity passing through it. The smallest fragments travel farthest from their original location in the gel. The gel is then stained with dyes to make bands of DNA visible, and a pattern is created. The location of a band within a pattern indicates which base pairs it contains.

Gel electrophoresis is used to provide genetic information for many purposes, from diagnosis of disease to suspect identification by police.

GLOSSARY

acid: A substance that reacts with water to form hydrogen ions. Acids are usually sour and corrosive materials.

alloy: Substance made from two or more metals or from a metal and a nonmetal.

amino acid: Small molecules that make up proteins and provide cells with the material they need to grow and maintain their structure.

anion: Negatively charged particle (ion) formed when an atom gains electrons.

atom: The smallest particle in an element that has the same chemical properties as the element.

bacteria: A group of single-cell organisms lacking chlorophyll and having a simple nucleus.

base (DNA): One of four nitrogen-containing compounds in DNA—the four bases are adenine (A), cytosine (C), guanine (G), and thymine (T). The order of bases tells the cell which proteins to make.

base (in chemistry): A substance that reacts with water to form hydroxide ions

(one atom of oxygen plus one atom of hydrogen).

bond (chemical): Attractive force between negatively charged electrons and positively charged protons that holds atoms together.

carbohydrate: Chemical made up of oxygen, hydrogen, and carbon, which is broken down into sugars in the body.

catalyst: A chemical that changes the rate of a reaction but is not changed itself during the reaction.

cation: Positively charged particle formed when an atom loses electrons.

cell membrane: Thin layer of proteins that surrounds a cell and gives it its shape—the membrane lets some, but not all, substances through.

chlorophyll: Green chemical in plants that absorbs light.

compound: A substance that contains atoms of more than one element joined together.

covalent bond: Bond in which atoms share an electron.

deoxyribose: A sugar molecule, which is present in DNA.

double bond: Two atoms bonded together by sharing two pairs of electrons.

double helix: The shape of a molecule of DNA—like a ladder twisted around itself.

DNA (deoxyribonucleic acid): Large molecules that contain all the instructions cells need to make proteins.

electron: Extremely small particle that orbits the nucleus of an atom—electrons have a negative electric charge.

element: Substance that cannot be broken down into simpler substances by chemical means—an element contains only one kind of atom.

endothermic reaction: A chemical reaction that takes in energy.

enzyme: Natural catalyst—enzymes speed up chemical reactions in living things.

exothermic reaction: Chemical reaction that gives off energy, such as heat.

fat: Type of lipid that is solid at room temperature. Lipids are stored in the body and used as a source of energy.

fructose: A type of sugar that occurs in fruit.

glucose: A type of sugar that contains six atoms of carbon. Glucose is also called blood sugar because it is transported in the blood.

indicator: Substance that changes color depending on the strength of an acid or a base added to it.

ion: Atom that has either lost or gained electrons.

ionic bond: Bond in which atoms transfer an electron.

lactase: The enzyme that breaks up the larger lactose molecule into glucose and galactose, simple sugars that the body can use.

lactose: Type of sugar that occurs in milk.

lipids: Group of chemicals that are greasy to the touch and soluble in alcohol but not in water—they include oils and fats.

mineral (in food): Substances that are needed by the body for it to function and are obtained from food. Iron, potassium, sodium, calcium, and magnesium are important minerals for people.

molecule: Group of atoms that share electrons—they are bonded together.

nucleus: The center of an atom—the nucleus contains protons and neutrons.

oil: Type of lipid that is liquid at room temperature.

organism: Any living thing.

organic chemistry: The branch of chemistry that deals with carbon and its compounds.

oxygen: Colorless, odorless element that makes up one-fifth of Earth's air as a gas.

pH (percent hydrogen) scale: Scale on which the strength of acids and bases is measured—a pH of 1 is the most acidic; a pH of 14 is the least acidic and is a strong base.

physical chemistry: The branch of chemistry that deals with the changes that occur during chemical reactions.

pigment: Substances in plant or animal cells that give them color. Also refers to colors in paint.

polymerase: An enzyme that cuts chains of molecules called polymers into smaller pieces (monomers).

protein: Chains of amino acids.

proteinase: A chemical that dissolves proteins.

reactants: Chemicals involved in a chemical reaction.

reaction: Any type of chemical change that involves electron movement.

single bond: Bond in which atoms are joined by sharing one pair of electrons.

solution: Liquid containing two or more substances.

starch: Carbohydrate found in plants such as rice, wheat, and potatoes.

sucrose: A simple sugar, also called table sugar.

sugar: Carbohydrate such as glucose, lactose, or fructose.

vitamin: Small molecules of carbon compounds needed by all except the most simple living things to grow and keep healthy.

yeast: Tiny, single-celled organism that converts sugars into carbon dioxide.

SET INDEX